Beatrie Banning Brooks

WEDDING EMBASSY YEAR BOOK

SEVENTH EDITION

Published annually by

THE WEDDING EMBASSY, INC.

341 MADISON AVENUE

NEW YORK

AN ANNOUNCEMENT BY MISS BRENNIG

PROSPECTIVE bride, perhaps you would like to know why your copy of my book comes to you from one of your city's leading stores rather than directly from The Wedding Embassy.

Nine years ago, I founded The Wedding Embassy. Nearly five years ago now, by popular demand, I wrote and published the first Wedding Embassy Year Book.

For each of the first two years 12,000 complimentary copies were sent to prospective brides. The third year 30,000 copies were distributed, and still the demand grew! — During 1938, a greatly enlarged circulation was made possible by the cooperation of one of the leading stores in your city (as well as other leading stores in other cities). Therefore, when possible will you not patronize the store through whom you received your copy of Wedding Embassy Book? I assure you that it merits your consideration.

As in the past, all advisory services of The Wedding Embassy, such as management, budgeting or counseling are without cost to the Bride and Groom and the wedding party. These services are obtainable through the Bridal Department of the store presenting this book to you.

☆ ☆ ☆

The Place to Go

FOR YOUR TROUSSEAU

THE rule of simplicity and good taste essential in all that pertains to this momentous event gives assurance to every bride-to-be that her own shall be a beautiful wedding and she the loveliest of brides. As this book is equally helpful to brides whose expenditures must be carefully budgeted and to those upon whom no such restrictions are imposed, so does the service of the

Strawbridge & Clothier Bridal Shop

meets the requirements of every bride in the matter of cost as well as of becoming elegance.

In addition to providing a wide selection of Dresses, Lingerie and everything included in the bride's trousseau, we are equipped to give expert, personal service in making every detail contribute to the perfection every bride has a right to expect.

So, however modest or ample the sum you wish to spend, *come directly to our* BRIDAL SHOP on the third floor. Here you will get helpful advice, whether your complete outfit be chosen without leaving this room, or the Dresses bought and fitted here, and the various accessories selected in their respective departments.

You'll find in the Bridal Shop a wide selection of Brides' Dresses, Veils, etc., and of Bridesmaids Dresses as well, with a number of private fitting-rooms adjoining.

Many customers find our Deferred Payment service
a welcome convenience in the purchase of wedding
Trousseaux. This may readily be arranged, if desired

STRAWBRIDGE & CLOTHIER
Market, Eighth and Filbert Sts., Philadelphia

*wishing you
a long life full of happiness.
Marie Coudert Bruning —*

MARIE COUDERT BRENNIG, daughter of Mrs. Dongan de Peyster and the late Baron Benno Frederic von Brennig; granddaughter of the late Charles Coudert, internationally known barrister, and niece of the late Duchess de Choiseul, has, it is obvious, the perfect social background for the business to which she now devotes her energy and her talents — the management of weddings. It is equally obvious, therefore, that what she says regarding weddings has the authority of background, plus specialized observation. Every detail of wedding plans described in her book has been actually supervised by Miss Brennig at some time during her many years of experience in assisting thousands of brides to the altar through her "Wedding Embassy." And, when she notes changes in traditional custom, she is in a position to judge of their advisability.

The modern wedding, with its complex arrangements, touches many groups. Miss Brennig, a true business woman, is aware of the immense ramifications of these modern social functions; and her book of wedding etiquette is the first to deal fully with the various aspects of the many types of business concerned with wedding arrangements.

During the past eleven years, people in all parts of the United States have turned to her for help in planning weddings. She is as much interested in the small wedding as in the large. Her book should be welcome and useful wherever there are brides — which is everywhere!

CONTENTS

☆ ☆ ☆

CONTENTS

CONTENTS

☆ ☆ ☆

THE BRIDE'S GIFT RECORD

This Record provides 180 entries and will be found at end of book

Your acknowledgment of the receipt of this book, and any comment you wish to make will be greatly appreciated

Marie Coudert Brening

Editor

CHAPTER I

The Place of Tradition

YOUR WEDDING! Not mine, nor the next door neighbor's — but Yours, Prospective Bride and Groom! Which means that financial and social problems peculiarly your own are to be considered in wedding plans — not anybody else's — your own desires and predilections are to be taken into consideration — not what other people want or think you should want.

It is from this point of view — your individual needs in making wedding plans — that I want to discuss your wedding with you. Tradition must be made to fit into your special problems, rather than your problems into tradition. Many of the questions that arise in connection with the modern wedding cannot be solved at all by adherence to strict traditional form. Yet they can be solved in a way that will fall within the bounds of the correct.

Among the thousand brides — and grooms — whom I have helped in planning for this all-important day in their lives, each couple has had problems different, in some aspect, from all the others. We have solved each problem according to individual needs. The thought of a wedding should inspire no awe. There are no hidebound rules that need make you wretched or involve you in too great expense. There are certain simple formalities, it is true, based upon convenience, the customs of the past, beauty, sentiment, that do not change, but within these simple limits, there is room for all the variation and latitude you may wish or require.

Your own locality, of course, determines many details in the wedding plans. If you live in Parr's Corners, Idaho, you will not try to carry out your wedding as if you were a resident of New York City. While you will want to adhere to certain forms, do not be afraid to follow local customs in many others. Courtesy, simplicity, unostentation — remember these and your wedding will be joyous for you and all your guests.

In this rapidly changing world, our concepts of wedding etiquette are by no means what they were a number of years ago. Changing modes of thought and changing ways of living have materially altered many traditional ideas.

Consider, for instance how, only a few years ago, it was actually considered undignified for a family with any claim to social prominence to hold their daughter's wedding reception anywhere else but in the family home. What a change today! The largest and most important receptions — and marriage ceremonies also — are held in hotels and clubs, and this is considered "quite the thing."

This change of attitude is very easy to understand. In nearly every city living accommodations, even among the wealthiest, are inadequate for the purposes of a large wedding. A comparatively small apartment has taken the place of the once spacious family residence; staffs of servants are proportionately smaller. So in most city homes a wedding of any size is entirely out of the question. Present-day conditions have altered earlier customs.

Not so long ago, a bride was expected to choose pure white for her formal wedding gown. Today in about seven out of ten cases, she selects one of the "off white" shades or even pastel shades, if she prefers. And no more does she contemplate putting her gown away in lavender, to show reverently, in her old age, to a younger generation. Our modern bride is a more practical soul, and she deliberately has her wedding gown designed so that it may later be altered into an evening gown — another reason why she may choose a tint instead of white.

Fashion once required that the ultra-correct wedding must be in June. But today October is nearly as popular, and smart weddings are held at almost any time of the year. The exigencies of business and the groom's vacation, the propensity for travel, which requires certain times of year for certain places, and many other changes have united to dissipate the idea of the "June Bride."

There are other problems of a more financial nature where you need not fear tradition. Let us take an example. It is always customary, of course, for the groom to remunerate the officiating clergyman. According to tradition, the fee is to be determined in proportion to the size of the wedding. But suppose a young man is marrying a girl with a great deal of money, who wants a large and elaborate wedding. How foolish it would be for him to refuse her this fine wedding because he cannot afford to give to the clergyman a fee proportionate to the size of the affair! His offering, of course, will have to be, and should be, in keeping with his financial position. His individual problem supersedes tradition. This seems — and is — the simple and natural solution; but this very problem, absurd as it may seem to the average person, is often heatedly discussed in the making of wedding plans.

Or let us take another example. Custom and tradition decree "Full dress" as correct for a gentleman to wear at a formal evening affair. Suppose the majority of a group of young college men, invited to be ushers at a formal evening wedding in the South — where a wedding at such an hour is quite "smart" — cannot afford to buy dress suits for that one occasion. Are they to be excluded from ushering at a friend's wedding because tradition requires them to wear full evening dress? They probably all have Tuxedos. Their youth and financial situation make their own problem supersede tradition within the realm of good taste. Of course, they must all be dressed exactly alike with correct accessories.

Yes, there are, of course, certain fundamental rules, which we shall discuss as we go on. But particular problems such as these we have just described may be made to fit into the correct way, creating a result that is dignified, simple and within the bounds of tradition.

So together, let us investigate.

CHAPTER II

Dignified Simplicity

"THE BRIDE wore a gown of white satin trimmed with flowers and orange blossoms; her veil, of Point de Venise lace, was secured by a diamond star and caught up by a large diamond butterfly. She also wore a cross and necklace of family jewels."

"The bride's mother, Mrs. William Astor, wore a yellow satin brocade gown, which glittered with diamonds. She also wore a diamond necklace and diamond leaves ornamented her hair."

So read a news story of half a century ago, when Miss Charlotte Augusta Astor became the bride of Mr. J. Coleman Drayton.

How times have changed! Today brides sparkling with jewels and "adorned like a Christmas tree" are found only in comic opera. Our present-day ideal is dignified simplicity; and to be "chic" and really lovely, Our Bride must be simply attired, with perhaps one small ornament of jewels, or none. "How simple and bride-like!" This is one of the truest compliments she can receive.

The same principle of simplicity applies to other details of the wedding. To maintain this ideal, however, does not mean that a wedding will not be beautiful and perfect in every way. But a perfect wedding has no earmarks of being overdone.

Unfortunately, and usually when expense does not have to be considered, it is all too easy to overdo. I recall an instance at a Spring home wedding — a large and elaborate affair. The chief decorations at the improvised altar in the ballroom were to be a pair of dogwood trees in full bloom, an ideal decoration for the season. Upon their arrival, the two trees turned out to be somewhat scantily equipped with blossoms, whereupon an enthusiastic florist, given carte blanche as to expense, ordered three hundred rhododendron blossoms to be wired on the dogwood branches! The result was sumptuous indeed, but it resembled nothing in heaven or on earth; and those masses of incongruous bloom completely spoiled the beauty and simplicity of the altar setting.

In a small country church, decorated for a fashionable wedding, I once viewed another startling result of this tendency to overdo. Down the full length of the main aisle of the simple little structure stretched a magnificent and luxuriant rose arbor, through which the bridal party must pass to the altar. So luxuriant was it indeed that the bridal party could scarcely be seen; and the lovely line and detail of the little church, a perfect setting for a wedding, were completely lost.

Brides who have all the money in the world to spend can very easily make the mistake also of overelaborateness in their wedding attire. One wealthy bride I knew chose exquisite white Duchesse satin for her wedding dress, the yoke and sleeves covered with pearl and rhinestone embroidery; with it she chose to wear a "Baby Stuart" type cap of the same embroidery. Somewhat elaborate, it is true, but considering the other features of the wedding, perfectly suitable and in good taste.

But in the family was a priceless lace veil — the property of Aunt Mary — and Aunt Mary was determined that the bride should wear this too! Now that *would* have been overdoing with a vengeance. I firmly stated that the wedding veil should, with such a gown and cap, be preferably of the simplest white tulle; had the family veil been used, the gown should have been extremely simple and practically untrimmed.

When Miss Anna Gould was married in the latter half of the last century, bits of wedding cake were packed in solid gold boxes. Today these souvenirs of the wedding are packed in plain white boxes bearing an engraved silver or gold monogram.

CHAPTER III

Formality and Informality

IT ALL DEPENDS upon what kind of a wedding Our Bride may wish. A simple muslin dress with a wide brimmed hat may be just as good form as a satin gown and veil; and delicious homemade ice cream quite as proper as "wedding bells in moulds."

The question is — shall the wedding be formal or informal? There is no such thing as semi-formal, when it comes to weddings; but there are degrees of formality and informality too; and formality or informality may be simple or elaborate.

After all, as an old aunt of mine used to say, "It isn't so much what you do as the way you do it, so long as details correspond." Within the limits of both formality and informality there is room for infinite variation and for initiative in ideas. An informal wedding may be as perfect in form, if you will excuse a little redundancy — as a formal wedding!

Automatically, of course, if Our Bride chooses to be married in a gown and veil, she prescribes for herself a "formal" wedding. Our Groom should then wear "formal" costume also — as should the other men in the wedding party — in other words, cutaways with formal accessories. This is very easy to understand. Generally speaking, how would a business suit or white flannel trousers and blue coat look beside a wedding gown and veil? In particular cases, however, exceptions to this rule may be made, and if the necessary details are carried out, the completed "picture" remains correct. For exceptions to this rule see page 130. It is all a matter of being consistent in detail. Certain formalities in service for the bridal feast, in seating, in guest procedure, belong merely to generally accepted forms, which are based, when it comes right down to basic facts — on the simplest rudiments of courtesy and appearance.

But if Our Bride decides to dispense with gown and veil, and attire herself just as becomingly — though perhaps not so romantically — in a lovely peach velvet afternoon gown with a train, and a matching hat, with veil, then her wedding is informal. However, the groom, in this case, will properly wear a cutaway to correspond with her gown. If Our Bride chooses a garden wedding, and wears a "garden party" costume with hat, Our Groom will wear a dark blue coat with white flannel trousers. The first of these weddings will represent, so to speak, the more formal type of informal wedding.

Toward the other extreme of the informal would be the wedding, perhaps at home, perhaps in a hotel or club, at which the bride would wear her traveling costume and the groom a business or traveling suit. Even more informal would be the wedding in which the pair go to a magistrate or to a rectory for the ceremony. The mountain wedding we shall describe in a later chapter typifies the most informal type of outdoor wedding.

A formal wedding, as the informal one, may be in a variety of places, at a variety of times, with a variety of detail as to costumes, music, flowers, refreshments and all other arrangements.

Perhaps if we were to attend in imagination a typical large formal church wedding, we might vision more clearly just what is meant by the "extreme" in formality. Later, we shall consider weddings of less formality. In this way we shall also understand the variety possible in informal weddings.

CHAPTER IV

I Am a Wedding Guest

THE LARGE formal wedding here described should be considered merely as a "pattern," representing a standard — stereotyped if you will — method of managing the wedding when there are no reasons to deviate from certain accepted forms or to economize in money or time. The prospective bride in a small village, for instance, will find here correct methods of procedure; but whenever and wherever this particular bride is to be married, she, or any other bride, may change these methods to suit her special needs. Such variations and adaptations to weddings of different sizes are discussed in later chapters.

Mr. and Mrs. Schuyler Warren Wood
request the honour of your presence
at the marriage ceremony of their daughter
Marie Louise
to
Doctor Martin Gordon Beverley
on Thursday, the tenth of June
at half after four o'clock
at Saint Giles Cathedral
New York City

Mr. and Mrs. Schuyler Warren Wood
request the pleasure of your company
on Thursday, the tenth of June
at five o'clock
at the Hotel Ascot

Kindly send response
to Eleven hundred Fifth Avenue

I have received one of the two thousand invitations which Mr. and Mrs. Schuyler Warren Wood have issued to the marriage ceremony of their daughter; and enclosed with it, one of the five hundred invitations to the wedding reception following.

It is now one month in advance of the wedding — the invitations have been sent out an unusually long time ahead, but it is to be a large affair and many guests are expected from a distance. The four weeks give me ample time to make plans to attend the reception, and of course I must reply as soon as possible. The bride's family will also have sufficient time to receive acceptances, or regrets, and then to plan accordingly for the wedding repast — a very important matter, since the caterer will charge so much per cover. Of course no answer is expected to the church invitation.

Having decided that I am also able to attend the reception, I send my acceptance thus:

> Miss Marie Coudert Brennig
> accepts with pleasure the kind invitation
> of
> Mr & Mrs Schuyler Warren Wood
> for their daughter's wedding reception
> on Thursday the tenth of June
> at five o'clock
> at the Hotel Ascot

If I had declined, I should have written:

> Miss Marie Coudert Brennig
> regrets that she is unable to accept
> Mr & Mrs Schuyler Warren Wood's
> kind invitation
> for their daughter's wedding reception
> on Thursday the tenth of June
> at five o'clock
> at the Hotel Ascot

I Offer a Gift

Once upon a time it was taken for granted that only intimate friends of the family were invited to wedding receptions; and whether they attended or not, they generally sent a gift. Today, when many mere acquaintances are invited to such functions, often for business as well as social reasons, the sending of a gift is not obligatory if the person invited does not attend, though it would be a generous gesture. But if one does accept the invitation, a gift is of course the correct procedure.

So, having accepted the reception invitation, I cogitate on the matter of my gift. I know it need not be costly, if my means do not permit. And of course, it must be sent to the bride — this even though I might know only the groom, and the present may be designed for the use of both!

Now it happens that I know Marie Louise quite well, and a few days later, as I meet her on the street, I ask her point-blank, "Marie Louise, which would you prefer, a silver vase or an etching?" She says, "Etching," so that is what I buy.

Had I not known her intimately, I might have consulted some of her friends as to her preferences. But after all, I need not take this matter of a gift too seriously. If I choose it thoughtfully and delicately, giving due attention to what I know of the tastes of the bride and groom, I cannot go far wrong anyway. In this instance, for example, I would under no circumstances select a cocktail shaker, since I happen to know both Marie Louise and Martin are teetotalers — and it is always simple for anyone to avoid making an unsuitable gift.

I dispatch the etching to Marie Louise's home two weeks in advance of the wedding; to wait longer would be to add unnecessary detail to her last days of preparation, for she should acknowledge her gifts immediately. Besides, too long a delay on my part would give the impression that the gift is a last minute thought. With the etching I enclose my engraved visiting card, my last name and the "Miss" crossed out, since we are old friends, and I write on the face of the card in ink "Wishing you much happiness." With a less intimate friend, I would simply enclose my card without any personal message.

Then comes, — to me at least, a very important question — my costume for the wedding.

Since I am feminine, my choice demands a little more detailed consideration than mere male attire. I want to be sufficiently elegant, but inconspicuous, as befits maturity; so I choose a rather dressy flowered material, made on somewhat tailored lines, with hat in keeping, gloves and all other suitable accessories. The younger girls whom I know will wear gayer colors and appropriate hats. The men of my acquaintance, I know, will wear the conventional cutaway coat of oxford tone cheviot, striped gray worsted trousers, white shirts and wing collars with black and gray ties, and top hats.

Finally the day of the wedding arrives, and comfortable in the consciousness of an appropriate and becoming gown, I betake myself to the church.

AT THE CHURCH

As I enter the vestibule of the church, I am transported swiftly into the fragrant and solemn atmosphere of the wedding. There is a hush of solemnity. The scent of flowers is in the air. I hear the soft strains of music.

An usher comes forward to meet me. He greets me politely, and asks, since he does not already know, "Are you a friend of the bride or of the groom?"

I answer that I am a friend of the bride, and I hand him my engraved pew card. He bows slightly, offers me his right arm, escorts me up the center aisle to my place on the left hand side, the customary side of the church for friends of the bride's family. I see members of the groom's family sitting on the right of the main aisle. I am delighted that my seat is about half way to the front, giving me a splendid view of the decorations and of the arrival of the guests; an ideal location, too, for viewing the wedding procession.

There is something mystical about a church adorned for a wedding. The lovely blossoms, the soft green foliage, create something of the atmosphere of the most majestic of all cathedrals. Nature's great woods. Light filters through the greenery over the stained glass windows; from the organ loft in the rear steal the soft strains of the organ with the accompaniment of a string quartet. I lean back and drink in the beauty of the scene.

About the front and side walls of the church stand lovely silver birches, their delicate white branches with silvery green leaves almost ethereal in their beauty. At intervals trees of flowering pink peach blossoms send their clusters halfway to the birches' tops. Garlands of greenery that lie over the windows give me the impression of gazing out into a deep woodland. The altar is massed with white peach blossoms, white lilac and Canterbury bells. Along the aisles are Canterbury bells and white iris.

I have been lost in a sort of pleasant reverie, but presently I become conscious of whisperings and rustlings around me, and I realize that the Cathedral is rapidly filling with the wedding guests, the ladies escorted to their seats always on the arm of an usher, their men escorts following behind. For those more distant acquaintances to whom engraved pew cards have not been sent, the rear seats are given. Gay young girls in light attire, older women in more subdued summer colors, the men in the usual cutaway — it is a pleasant picture. There is much animated nodding of heads and a subdued whispering as friends and relatives who have not seen each other for a long time exchange their greetings. For a wedding is also very much a reunion!

Now a lady with graying hair who is most attractively gowned in blue passes slowly up the aisle on an usher's arm, followed by a dignified gray-haired gentleman. When they are ushered into the front pew on the right hand side, I realize that they must be the father and mother of the groom. A few other late guests are seated; I know that it must be very near the hour for the ceremony, and I hope there will not be too many late comers.

There is a little hush of expectancy, and all heads turn as a charming matron in gown of rose beige with hat to match, wearing a corsage of orchids, moves slowly to the front of the church on an usher's arm. It is the bride's mother; and I know the other guests are thinking with me, "What a young woman to have a daughter of marriageable age!" She is ceremoniously seated in the front pew on the left hand side.

Two ushers now come forward and stretch white ribbons along the pews on either side of the center aisle, starting from a point about one quarter of the way back to and including the last pew, so that guests will remain seated after the ceremony until members of the immediate family have been escorted from the church. Then there is a triumphant chord from the organ — and the strains of the Lohengrin Wedding March begin.

The Pageant of the Protestant Wedding

Here comes the Bride! The congregation rises as one. I can see the entire bridal procession as it moves slowly up the aisle toward the altar.

First come the ushers, — eight of them, walking in pairs, evenly spaced, about six feet apart. They are the pace makers for the wedding procession. Identical in appearance, each wears the formal attire for an afternoon wedding in June — a cutaway coat of oxford tone cheviot; medium tone striped gray worsted trousers, double breasted pearl gray linen waistcoat, pearl gray suede gloves, "bat wing" collar with black and pearl gray striped four-in-hand tie, shirt with stiff cuffs, black oxfords, spats of pearl gray. Each has a gardenia boutonnière.

Another interval of eight feet — and the bridesmaids, each pair six feet from the pair in front. What a lovely picture! They are wearing white chiffon form-fitting gowns, with skirts to the floor and short sleeves; each pair has accessories of a different color. Thus the first two have around their wide-brimmed horsehair hats, turned off the face, ribbons of daffodil yellow, their slippers are of the same color, and the ribbons that tie their bouquets of white sweet peas are also yellow. They wear long white suede gloves. The second pair have accessories of pale fern green; the third, sunset peach, the fourth, Madonna blue.

Again, an interval of about eight feet — and the maid of honor. She too is dressed like the bridesmaids, with the exception of her accessories, which are white. But on her bouquet instead of one color, there is a shower of ribbons of all the colors in the costumes of the eight bridesmaids, so that she seems to bring the whole color scheme together.

At last, leaning lightly on her father's right arm, perhaps eight feet behind the maid of honor, comes Marie Louise, Our Bride, cynosure of all eyes. She makes a picture we shall not soon forget.

Her wedding gown is of white mousseline de soie, snugly fitting her lovely slender figure. At the neck the gown opens in a wide square; the sleeves are long and tight; she wears no gloves; her slippers match her gown.

Her veil, of the same material as her gown — this is an unusual idea, but very lovely — is held in place by a satin band about her head, the band being covered by throwing back the upper portion of the veil — a nun-like effect, which is very becoming. The veil itself reaches to the end of her five yard train. Her wedding bouquet is white spray orchids in a double cluster, combined with lilies of the valley, the ribbon matching the tone of her gown.

Slowly, with dignity, the pairs of ushers and bridesmaids are dividing at the chancel steps, four of the ushers taking their places on either side, with four bridesmaids in front of them. The groom has entered from the vestry, accompanied by his best man, and stands at the right of the steps awaiting the bride. He is dressed exactly like the ushers, save that he wears a pearl gray ascot tie, and his boutonnière is a spray of lilies of the valley, probably from the bride's bouquet. The best man is similarly attired, with a gardenia in his buttonhole.

As the bride approaches, the groom hands to the best man his gray gloves. Marie Louise withdraws her hand from her father's arm, slips her bouquet from her right arm to her left, and puts her hand through the left arm of the groom. Her father maintains his position back of his daughter, a little to the left. The maid of honor has taken her place in front of the brides-maids, to the left of the bride.

The beautiful Episcopal marriage service now begins, read by the clergyman in his impressive voice. When he reaches the question, "Who giveth this woman to be married to this man?", the father steps forward, takes Marie Louise's right hand, and extends it to the groom or minister (this custom varies in different churches). Then he retires to the front pew beside his wife.

Now the clergyman slowly and solemnly ascends the steps to the candle-lighted altar. The bride and groom follow, the maid of honor and the best man behind them, taking their places on the left and right as before. The remainder of the wedding party wait in their places at the chancel steps. As they thus group themselves, music plays softly, and continues a barely audible accompaniment throughout the remainder of the ceremony. The bride hands her bouquet to the maid of honor during the period of the ring service.

I observe that at the proper time the best man, removing his right glove, takes from his pocket the wedding ring and hands it to the clergyman, who in turn gives it to the groom.

"With this ring I thee wed," says the groom; the minister concludes the ceremony; they are man and wife. We are all standing quietly as the final blessing is asked, then we hear the incomparable Mendelssohn wedding march. The minister extends his congratulations, and the bride and groom

[23]

turn for the recessional. The maid of honor, handing her own bouquet to one of the bridesmaids as she comes to the chancel steps, stoops briefly to adjust the bride's train — her ancient office; then takes back her own bouquet and follows on the arm of the best man. Two by two, an usher and a bridesmaid together form the remainder of the wedding party in the triumphant recessional. Happy faces of bride and groom, pride in each other, gladness at the thought of life together — it all leaves us joyful, yet with a mist in our eyes!

While the ushers return, to escort to their cars, with great formality, first the mother of the bride, then the mother of the groom, and other immediate members of both families, we who are not members of the immediate family, being hemmed in by ribbons, sit quietly until all the relatives have left; then the ushers take away our satin barrier and we go on to the reception.

AT THE RECEPTION

Having joined some friends on my way out of the church, I ride with them to the hotel where the reception is taking place. I find that one of the large ballrooms is being used for the occasion. From the doorway, as I enter, the effect of the decorations is indescribably lovely. The bridal party has taken its place in a long receiving line. Music is playing softly from somewhere behind the screen of green; the atmosphere is no longer full of mystery but gay and lively, with a pleasant hum of conversation and cheerful bursts of laughter.

To the announcer stationed near the bride's mother I give my name, and he repeats it audibly to her. For, as hostess, she is first to greet the guests. I shake hands cordially with her; then with the father of the groom, who stands next in line; with the mother of the groom, and the father of the bride; and finally with the bride herself. I kiss her affectionately and I say," Marie Louise, I hope you will always be as happy as you are today."

She presents her new husband to me, saying, "Martin, Marie Brennig is one of my oldest friends. . . ." We shake hands, he murmurs, "Thank you."

I then offer a brief greeting to the maid of honor who stands on the right of the groom, also speaking a word to the bridesmaids. A continual stream of guests precedes and follows me; many of the men claiming laughingly their privilege of kissing the bride. Occasionally an usher, still on duty even here, politely escorts an elderly man or woman to the receiving line. I, having completed my greetings, proceed into an adjoining room where the wedding repast is being served.

Since this is an unusually large reception, arrangement has been made for buffet service; this table, set at one side of the room, shows off to great advantage the lovely peach blossoms, white lilacs and greenery. In leisurely fashion, chatting meanwhile with friends, seated at one of the small tables grouped in friendly fashion about the ballroom, I enjoy my cold bouillon, lobster salad, tiny assorted sandwiches, ice cream in the form of a wedding bell, and a demitasse.

It seems a comparatively short time until the bride and groom, leaving the receiving line, pass by us on their way to the bridal table, arranged for them and their party in an adjoining room. I see it through the doorway. Low vases of jasmine and white sweet peas adorn it; and in the center is the lovely bride's cake. Before it the bridal pair take their places, she on his right; and in the usual order, the best man on the right of the bride, then the bridesmaids and ushers alternately; on the groom's left sits the maid of honor. At another smaller table are the parents of the pair, the officiating clergyman and his wife, and a few members of the immediate families. I catch a glimpse of the bride as she laughingly cuts the first piece of bride's cake; in accordance with immemorial custom, it is served to the groom first.

Near the door of the ballroom, a special table has been arranged with small monogrammed boxes of wedding cake, a souvenir for each guest. An attentive butler presides over this, and it is just as well, I know, for it is a great temptation to any guest to take more than one home to a relative who could not attend! The wedding gifts are not being shown here; a tea to view them was given at the bride's home yesterday.

The orchestra has now emerged from its seclusion, and is playing dance music; and couples are circling about the floor. Other groups are sitting or standing. None of us wish to leave until the bride and groom have left for their honeymoon!

They must take a steamer, it seems, which sails at midnight, so it is not long before the bridal party reappears. Just as the bride reaches the door of the ballroom, she turns and throws her bouquet among the laughing bridesmaids, and as they gaily seek to catch it, she and the groom "vanish" to their suite to change into their "going-away" costumes.

At last the bride and groom step from the elevator. How pretty she looks in her simple and becoming costume! The goodbyes to her family and to his have been said upstairs; no time for formalities now; they dash out the door; we follow them and hurl our paper rose leaves; they enter their car and are off.

No white ribbons stream behind as they drive away. The old shoes tied on the cars of newly-weds, I am diverted to recall, are the modern version of the missiles which, in ancient times, were hurled after a lucky warrior and his captive bride. But this is a big city wedding, and we have not embarrassed the bridal pair by such decorations, which might be perfectly suitable in a smaller community. However, they have had a fine send-off, as the rose leaves strewn on the pavement testify; and we go happily home.

CHAPTER V

Behind the Scenes

As an average guest at a wedding (such as just described) and if I had never had to manage one, I would perhaps be conscious only of the whole general perfection. But since I am one of those who know the "mechanics" of the wedding plans, so to speak, I can picture a succession of many happenings behind the scenes — the best man, rushing about to be sure that the groom is produced on time at the church, is only one of the many "performers."

I can even picture the possibility of having to pack the bride in ice before the wedding ceremony — if the day is very hot and she is very nervous! Many a bride has been enabled to go calmly through the marriage ceremony just because a wise mother or friend made her lie down for a time beforehand with an ice cap on her head!

Then, at the bride's home, I can imagine the butler giving careful last minute instructions to all the servants so that each one has his place and the wants of every guest will be provided for. I can picture the florist leaving the most delicate of the decorations until the very last minute, even at the risk of having to whisk ropes of smilax or wisps of fern from under the very footsteps of early arrivals — but assuring, in this way, that everything is fresh and sweet.

Outside the church, during the arrival of the guests and later during the ceremony, there is the carriage man, giving to the chauffeurs of arriving cars "return checks" so that they will line up in the proper order when the ceremony is over. It is his responsibility that the bride and groom will find their car waiting when they come from the church; with the cars of their wedding party following in the correct order — the bridesmaids, the bride's father and mother; the groom's father and mother; the nearest relatives and the ushers.

Or there is the sexton at the church door, charged perhaps with the great responsibility of the groom's hat and stick, a very important duty — but much perturbed, poor man, because everyone is asking him questions he cannot answer for he is frequently considered a kind of lady-in-waiting to the wedding party! Or I can imagine the ushers hastening breathlessly from their respective businesses so that they will be at the church at least an hour before the ceremony, only to find that early as they may be, there is always some guest earlier yet, who, having managed to effect an entrance, is of course sitting in the wrong pew, and must be politely requested to move!

As the moment for the ceremony approaches, I know that in the vestibule there is a last minute rush of late arrivals, just as the doors are being closed after the arrival of the bride's mother, the last guest to take her place. These late arrivals must be tactfully persuaded to use gallery or perhaps the side aisles — unfortunately they do not always seem to realize that entering the main aisle at this time will disturb the solemnity of the ceremony!

I know the ushers are mopping their brows, after their tasks, in an effort to compose themselves hastily before taking their places at the head of the wedding procession as it forms behind the closed doors.

Later at the wedding reception, when it is time for the bride and groom to go away, I know that the thoughtful bride will call her father and mother to her room to say a quiet goodbye, and also the father and mother of the groom — a gentle courtesy that she should not forget.

It is such little things as these that help to make the perfect wedding. What goes on "behind the scenes" is just as important as the "performance" itself.

CHAPTER VI

Variations

WE HAVE now seen, from start to finish, the arrangements for a typical formal wedding, which, in this instance, happened to take place in a church. It might quite properly have taken place in an apartment, a hotel or a restaurant. Infinite variations are possible in all other details. The same is true of the informal wedding, so called, as we have said, when the bride does not wear a formal wedding gown and veil.

Mr. and Mrs. Schuyler Warren Wood sent out the invitations for their daughter's formal wedding four weeks before the event. Three weeks would have been quite as correct, and two weeks would have been possible, though that gives too little time really to both guests and family. Only in cases of great emergency would engraved invitations be sent out less than two weeks before the ceremony.

Such a formal wedding could have taken place at twelve o'clock, or at twelve-thirty, as well as at half after four, though, of course, the latter is the more fashionable hour. Or if circumstances had demanded, it could have been at four or even at three-thirty. In the South it might have been in the evening and still have been quite correct. Then, of course, the members of the wedding party and the guests would have worn full evening attire.

At a home or hotel formal wedding there could be no ushers or only one or two depending on its size. At a church, instead of guests presenting reserved pew cards, the ushers could have typewritten lists of those to be seated in the reserved pews.

And the procession, too, can be infinitely varied, according to the number and character of the bridal party. There could be only a maid of honor and no bridesmaids, or, on the other hand, there could be both a maid and matron of honor as well as bridesmaids! And had Our Bride wished, she could have gone to the altar at her father's left side, holding his left arm, as an added tribute to her family, thus affording a better view of her gown, etc. This would have meant just a little more rehearsing the night before the wedding, and possibly she would have had to proceed further into the chancel so that her father could successfully avoid her train as he took his seat beside her mother.

Or, if she had had no father, she could have gone to the altar on the arm of an elder brother, or an uncle, or she could even go to the altar alone, if her father were deceased, and if, out of sentiment, she were unwilling that anyone should take his place. Her mother then could give her away, stepping from her pew when the minister said — "Who Giveth this Woman. . . .?"

In many a church with a gallery and steps leading down to the main body, a charming variation of the wedding procession is to have the bride and her attendants coming from the gallery. Various arrangements of the interior of churches make many changes possible in the wedding procession. The space between members of the bridal party will, of course, vary with the length of the aisle. White ribbons may or may not be used along the aisle where guests are seated.

And in the recessional, it is just as often customary for the ushers to walk two by two, and the bridesmaids in the same order, rather than by couples as in the wedding we have just described. Personally I consider the change made by allowing the bridesmaids and ushers to walk together is welcome from the point of view of variety in the wedding procession; it sets off the bridesmaids' costumes, and is a little compliment to the ushers besides!

Again, at the reception, we might not have a regular, full receiving line. Instead, the mother of the bride and the mother of the groom could receive nearer the entrance to the room, with the bridal party in the background. However, I always feel that the full receiving line is much the simpler and more gracious procedure; for surely, if guests are not willing to go to the effort of greeting the entire wedding party, when they have been invited and feasted and entertained, then they should not have come at all!

When a ceremony is held in a home, or a hotel, restaurant or club, naturally the reception will immediately follow in the same place. Guests may or may not be seated at a wedding repast, if it is in the form of a "high tea"; at a wedding breakfast seating is customary.

As we shall see later, music may vary widely both as to selections and musicians, though the use of the two usual wedding marches, the Lohengrin for the processional, the Mendelssohn for recessional, remains practically unaltered.

CHAPTER VII

Devotion to Detail

WHEN trifles annoy, we often reflect — it is the little things in life that count! Yes — and the little things in weddings!

Lack of attention to detail has caused havoc on many a wedding day. A collar button may be an infinitesimal thing, but I once attended a wedding ceremony that was delayed twenty minutes because the groom could not find that very necessary adjunct to his costume; agitation reigned supreme within his chambers, to say nothing of an awkward situation at the church where waited a distracted bride! And all because no one thought of the little detail of providing an extra button in case of emergency.

Whether a wedding be large or small, there are infinite minutiae, which may never occur to the uninitiated, but must receive attention for perfection of the whole.

Hose that perversely develop a run as the bride is arraying herself in her finery can nearly spell tragedy. But if she has had the thoughtfulness to purchase two pairs of the wedding hose instead of one, such an emergency brings no embarrassment.

A ribbon may seem an unimportant matter, but the whole effect of many a beautiful ensemble has been spoiled when the ribbon on a bridal bouquet is of a different tone from that of the wedding gown. It is not enough to say to a florist, "My gown is an off-white shade." How much off? There are many off-white shades; and he should be given a sample of the material so that he can match it exactly. If the gown is a pastel shade, this detail is all the more important. The same necessity applies to the ribbons along the aisle through which the party must pass.

No bride, of course, would ever knowingly wear an unbecoming gown and veil. Yet how many do! A pretty little plump bride wants a mediaeval gown because her friend "looked so beautiful in one on her wedding day." But her friend was tall and stately, and the mediaeval style suited her to perfection; on a small plump person, certain styles look merely ridiculous. A chin strap, which many brides fancy makes them look romantic, may indeed make a long, thin face look rounder and more youthful; to a plump face it merely gives the appearance of an animated cherub.

A wrinkled wedding gown! It is unthinkable. But unfortunately possible if the little detail of its proper care is overlooked. Unless the bride has an adequate space in her home to hang the gown at full length until the wedding day, it is far wiser to leave it at the shop until the last possible minute. And if it comes to the house packed in a box, it should be opened at once.

To a home where I was once arranging a wedding, the bride's wedding gown was delivered in a box several days in advance of the event, and a servant put the parcel carefully away unopened! Naturally when the gown was taken out a few days later, it was frightfully creased. Nor was that the worst. A nervous maid undertook to press it, and scorched a place along the train. By the time I arrived, the entire family was on the verge of hysteria. It was too late to make any drastic change; so I took some of the orange blossoms from the veil, sewed them over the yellowed place — and the day was saved! But to the bride, I know, it was tragic to wear, on that Day, a costume marred in the slightest detail; and the whole situation was very trying to everyone.

Details in the receiving of guests are also most important. Top hats, for instance, alike as so many peas, should have careful arrangements made for their checking. Likewise the care of wraps at a large wedding must be provided for. It is not conducive to the good nature of a guest to lose her best fur piece because she came to see her friend's daughter married!

A definite place for everything on the day of the wedding — and everything in its place — is most vital to the smoothness of the general effect. The groom must always have a place to change into his traveling clothes. Guests should have adequate retiring rooms for their use. A sufficient number of servants or assistants to the family should be on hand to answer questions and direct guests.

One of the most important items in the wedding plans is the guest list. Compiled carefully — preferably in a loose leaf notebook, or in a card file — and in alphabetical order, it will obviate many an uneasy qualm as to whether this person or that has been overlooked in sending out the invitations. A separate list should be kept for the ceremony and the reception — if the two affairs are to be in different places with a different number of guests. The preparation of this list should begin on the very day the wedding date is set and frequent conferences of the members of both families should assure that it is absolutely complete, so there will be no injured feelings anywhere.

Rehearse, rehearse, rehearse! This is the slogan of the night before a large wedding in which there is to be a considerable size bridal party. It is also the key to the effectiveness of the wedding procession. The rehearsal should take place where the ceremony is to be held; the whole wedding party should be present.

Brides — at least brides of my acquaintance — take part in the rehearsal

themselves, and do not leave this to an understudy. For they are not fool-
ishly superstitious and they do not think it will bring bad luck. And how
much nervous strain it saves on the actual wedding day!

At the rehearsal, ushers and bridesmaids should determine their places for
the morrow, the shorter ones preceding the taller. Starting in step from the
vestibule is difficult, but made easier if everyone will step out with the left
foot. The organist himself should make sure that he can bring his music to a
natural sounding close at the right moment — when the bride and groom
meet at the chancel steps facing the clergyman.

CHAPTER VIII

Setting the Stage

WHEN, WHERE, AND HOW

HERE are the four questions which Our Bride-to-be must first consider; upon her answers depend all the other details of her bridal plans.

1. What season of the year?
2. At home, in a church, hotel, restaurant, club?
3. Morning, afternoon or evening?
4. Formal or informal?

Whether her friends will be in town and able to attend her wedding is of more importance to her usually than the selection of any special month. Of course she may have decided preferences for a certain season; if she does not like cold weather, she will assuredly choose a summer wedding, and the reverse is true. But October today, as we have said, is just as "smart" as June for a town wedding; and any month at all may be considered, other factors being equal. Of course a Catholic wedding cannot take place in a church during Lent; nor would a large Episcopal wedding, while in many other Protestant churches a wedding at this time is not usually solemnized because of the general cessation of social events during a season of ecclesiastical mourning.

The hotel and club wedding, usually more or less elaborate and formal, comes under somewhat the same restrictions as the church affair. A quiet home wedding, formal or informal, might be celebrated at any time. A garden wedding, naturally, in northern climes, could not well be earlier than June first nor later than September fifteenth; but in the far south and in California it might conceivably be held at almost any time save during a rainy season.

THE TIME OF DAY

A wedding is usually planned for early morning, that is, eight or nine o'clock, only for some reason such as the necessity for early departure on the honeymoon; and such a wedding is generally informal, the bride wearing a simple gown and hat or traveling costume, the groom in business suit; there may be no attendants or only one or two. At this hour they may quite properly have a regular "sure enough" breakfast, a little elaborated, perhaps, to fit the occasion — fruit, egg soufflé, rolls, and coffee. A great many of the Catholic weddings held in a church with a nuptial mass, take place around ten o'clock in the morning.

High noon or half past twelve o'clock is a fashionable hour for what is termed the "morning wedding." Whether the wedding is formal or informal, it usually involves the serving of a wedding breakfast. In a formal morning wedding, the bride, of course, will wear her wedding gown and veil and the groom a cutaway or morning coat, just as in the afternoon. But if she chooses to be married in an afternoon gown and hat, or going away costume, her wedding, as we have said, becomes "informal." At this hour also there is, of course, the same latitude as to the number of wedding attendants.

Most fashionable of all, as we have seen in our story of the Beverley-Wood wedding, is the afternoon affair at half past four o'clock. We know what this requires in type of costume. But of course the afternoon wedding, too, may be informal, with the bride in afternoon gown and hat, and the groom in cutaway or dark suit — depending of course on the degree of informality.

In the East the evening wedding is not considered fashionable; but in the South, because of climate, and in some parts of the West, it is considered quite correct. If it is formal, that is with the bride wearing veil and wedding gown, all present should be in complete evening attire, both men and women. Usually the bride's attendants will not wear hats, though it is possible that some kind of headdress might be a part of their costumes. Such a formal evening wedding usually takes place about half past eight o'clock, though many a Southern wedding takes place at seven or half past. A real wedding supper may be served, or there may be lighter refreshments.

However, an evening wedding can be informal too, with the bride perhaps in simple dinner gown and evening-type hat, or in traveling costume; and the groom in dinner clothes. Here, too, a supper could be served; or there might simply be refreshments.

Place of the Wedding

It is not too much to say that most brides yearn to be married in church. It seems to give that sacred touch to a wedding that comes from no other environment, and to lend sanctity to the marriage tie.

But a large church, or even a moderately sized one, costs considerably to decorate. To make a church auditorium into the semblance of a chapel is also an undertaking for a florist and means considerable expense. A small chapel may be used, and of course here is the ideal for the small formal or informal wedding; and decorations may be modest. Brides who live in country homes during the summer often have delightful weddings in their little country church at a minimum of expense, with the added advantage that many of their friends are usually in the vicinity.

Next to a church, a home wedding is perhaps best beloved by brides. An old-fashioned house is a beautiful background for the bridal picture. But a large apartment is often quite as fine a setting, while even the modest two or three room apartment, or even one room, can be lovely; and a little cottage is adorable! We shall discuss later the floral decorations for the home, and the music, and the wedding repast. The simplest home wedding has an intimate charm that many other weddings lack.

Hotels and restaurants these days take weddings so much as a matter of course that they usually keep canopies and altars on hand. A small ballroom can be made to look quite like a chapel. To have the ceremony and wedding reception under one roof is a great advantage and a saver of time and expense.

For those not familiar with the use of hotels and clubs for such purposes, it might be said that generally no charge for space is made when a wedding menu is served.

Garden Weddings

It was late afternoon in midsummer. On the shores of the Sound lay a simple formal garden, gay with the colorful flowers of August. Beneath the shadow of the garden wall stood an improvised altar, stately with gold embroidered white cloth, bearing two branching candelabra and vases of white jasmine and lilies of the valley; before it a smilax-draped kneeling-bench in white. Leading to the altar a carpeted way was bordered by aisle posts trimmed with golden banded lilies. A small orchestra played softly as half a hundred guests gathered, some occupying the small chairs scattered about the garden, others standing under the spreading trees that bordered its edge.

Then the strains of the Lohengrin Wedding March, and through a trellised gateway came a bridal party. A tiny girl in Kate Greenaway costume of white dotted mull, with dainty poke bonnet, holding a little flower bouquet, another, a trifle taller, and then a third, taller still — the three little sisters of the bride, serving as her flower girls. Now followed the maid of honor, in Madonna blue, with hat to match, carrying a great sheaf of peach and blue flowers. And finally, on her father's arm, the bride herself, in a cream white satin close fitting gown, wearing a lace cap from which a long tulle veil floated behind her, passed slowly between the lilies to meet her young groom at the altar.

While the birds sang and musical wavelets lapped the shore, the white-robed clergyman read the marriage service, and another young pair started on the road of life together.

Afterwards, in the small patio adjoining the garden, under the shade of a spreading tree, the guests greeted the newly wedded couple. Then all proceeded to the lawn beside the water, where, under a marquee, small tables spread with white linen and adorned with late summer flowers, invited them to partake of the wedding repast. At a horseshoe-shaped table, dainty with vases of jasmine and lilies of the valley, sat the bridal party, before them a small table bearing the bride's cake. Perhaps a hundred guests partook of the delicious repast; and many enjoyed dancing on the specially built dance floor at the end of this same marquee, until time for the bridal pair to leave on their wedding trip.

Just a typical present-day garden wedding, this — more elaborate than some, more simple than others; but of a kind that is growing increasingly frequent in these days of simplicity and love of the out-of-doors. Certainly there is nothing more exquisite than a wedding ceremony under the trees and sky. The simplest garden, the tiniest lawn, may make a perfect setting. A garden scanty in bloom may be "dressed up" for the occasion by special planting; and roses can even be wired on rose bushes which have not seen fit to bloom in time!

Of course there is one drawback to the outdoor wedding — the uncertainty of weather in most parts of our country. The only way to deal with this difficulty is by making two wedding plans instead of one — in other words, one for out-of-doors, the other in case the ceremony must take place indoors. Since the house is usually decorated anyway, it requires very little extra expense or trouble to arrange a bower in a corner of the drawing or living room; and then it will be ready for emergency.

By no means does a bride always wear a formal white gown for a garden wedding. She is much more likely to wear a more informal filmy gown and a hat, perhaps white, perhaps of a pastel color if she prefers; with attendants in gay colors and hats also, and the men of the wedding party in white flannel trousers and dark blue coats. There may or may not be ushers. There is as much latitude possible in the garden wedding as in any other type, and it can be simplicity itself. If the bride does not wear wedding gown and veil, it of course becomes an "informal" wedding.

I recall a wedding of this kind that was utterly charming.

It took place in a small country village, in the simple informal garden behind one of those old-fashioned houses which has at the rear a high gallery porch over a brick terrace. The bride herself greeted the guests as they arrived, for all were her dearest friends and relatives. From the gallery they passed down into the garden.

Half past three had been chosen for the ceremony because the shadows were loveliest then. The only music was the rippling of the brook at the foot of the garden as the bride stepped out on the gallery, down the wooden steps and onto the flagged walk which led around the sundial toward the flowered garden border. She wore the same simple blue and white organdy in which she had received her guests, her head uncovered to show her bright blonde hair, and she carried a simple bouquet of blue azuretum and white phlox. Meantime, coming from the lower entrance of the house, the groom, in white flannel trousers and blue coat, and the clergyman, robed in white, passed together diagonally across the lawn and met her by the flowered hedge. After the simple ceremony, bride and groom walked to the other end of the garden, and the friends who greeted them all wrote their names in the white prayer book which the minister had used — a special souvenir of the occasion.

A simple wedding menu was served on the gallery, of consommé, chicken salad, sandwiches, ice cream, and coffee, all homemade, and the bride cut her cake which contained favors for everyone; to each guest was given a piece of this cake wrapped simply in white tissue paper. As the sun was setting, the bridal pair having changed into their going-away attire, drove off for a motor honeymoon, the bride, as a final gesture, throwing her bouquet from the car.

I remember another — and still simpler — outdoor wedding. It took place in April, in the front yard of a mountain cabin in the Blue Ridge Mountains. Great regiments of dogwood in full bloom crowded into the very doorway of the cabin. The bride was a beautiful, pink-cheeked young thing, in a frock of sheer white mull — perhaps from some cross-roads store, but on her it was a costume to dream of! The groom, a stalwart young mountain preacher, with fine eyes and an engaging smile, wore a "boughten-suit" of cheap black. But clothes were unimportant; it was the way those two splendid creatures looked at each other that made that wedding a beautiful and holy thing, as they stood under the canopy of dogwood trees to pledge their vows. Even fifty-thousand dollar weddings fade into insignificance when that picture comes back to me.

The Home Wedding

To many a bride, it is unthinkable to have her wedding anywhere but at home. She wants to take this important step in life in the midst of all her dearest associations. And if she lives in a charming old-fashioned house with a winding staircase, and fine spacious rooms, one might say that it would be almost a mistake to be married anywhere else!

However, as we have said before, almost any attractively furnished home, be it large or small, can be a charming setting for a wedding if plans are rightly made. Loving hands can turn the simplest surroundings into a bower of beauty for the great event.

It is only in a home, usually, that Our Bride can perform in the most perfect way that ceremony which has come to be thought of as peculiarly a part of weddings — throwing her bouquet from the stairway as she ascends to change into her traveling costume. This is one of the prettiest customs in wedding procedure — and it makes a picture that perhaps lingers longest in the memories of wedding guests. It is reminiscent of a custom in ancient Roman times, when the bride, having kindled the hearth fire in her new home from the marriage torch which had lighted the wedding procession homeward, flung the torch among the guests. Moreover a stairway in an old-fashioned house makes a setting of distinction and beauty for the wedding procession, and an ideal background for the bride, as she comes down it stately in her bridal gown, with her veil floating behind her.

If the house is sufficiently large, there can be a wedding procession just as in the church, though there will usually not be as many attendants, nor will the spacing between the members of the wedding party be as great. Sometimes an aisle formed by flower-decorated aisle posts marks off the path for the bridal party. If the ceremony requires it, an improvised altar is easily arranged; a small table covered with a white cloth, white flowers and perhaps candlesticks or candelabra adequately serves the purpose.

Unlike the church wedding, however, the home ceremony is not usually followed by a recessional, but the bride and groom, after the benediction is pronounced, turn from the officiating clergyman to receive their guests. The receiving line may be less formal than in the case of a hotel or club wedding.

Simplicity in detail, in decoration, in music, in wedding repast, is the best rule for the home wedding. Nor is any home, entirely denuded of its furnishings until it looks like a rented ballroom, ever as attractive a setting as when it retains as many as possible of its familiar and attractive features. How many of the usual furnishings can be left in place depends of course upon the size of the home, and the number of guests; but keeping home as home, even for a wedding, is important for every bride to remember.

For the ceremony, guests may be seated, or they may stand, with chairs enough, of course, so that those who are not able to stand, may be comfortable.

The wedding repast will usually be served necessarily in the dining room or in some other room than that in which the ceremony is performed. Arrangements should always be made, as at any other wedding reception, for guests to have retiring rooms in which to leave their wraps. In later chapters on music and flowers, we shall discuss these aspects of the wedding plans as they affect the home wedding. In planning for this type of ceremony, there are just as many possibilities and variations as in any other kind of wedding. Whether home be a great house, or a cottage, a magnificent apartment or a single room, the wedding ceremony held there can still be a thing of beauty and charm.

CHAPTER IX

The Catholic Nuptial Mass

A CEREMONIAL unsurpassable for sublimity and dignity is the Nuptial Mass of the Catholic Church. Only at the wedding of those being married for the first time may the Nuptial Mass be celebrated. It varies from the usual high Catholic mass in having special prayers for the bridal pair and a special ritual.

The Solemn Nuptial Mass, with full choir and all the panoply of Catholic ritual requires three priests for its celebration, each singing part of the mass, — a celebrant, a deacon and a subdeacon. For more than an hour, amid the mystery of swinging censers, the beauty of lighted candles on the altar, and the chanting of priests and the responses of the choir, this mass continues, throwing about the marriage a majesty and significance approached by no other ceremony. Obviously it is used only in the case of a large and elaborate wedding.

But there are two other types of Nuptial Mass quite as often celebrated — the low mass, which takes but half an hour, celebrated by one priest; and the high mass, or "missa cantata," much of which is sung, as the name indicates, and which requires perhaps forty minutes. (It should be remembered, however, that many Catholic weddings are celebrated in the church without any mass at all, merely with the simplest marriage ceremony; this type usually takes place in the afternoon.)

Most fashionable Catholic weddings, celebrated with a mass, take place at noon. Ten o'clock in the morning, however, is a common time, though a low mass is generally said at such times. And there are often weddings at eight or nine. Always before marriage, possibly the day before or the morning of the wedding, the parties to the marriage go to confession and partake of Holy Communion. If Holy Communion is partaken of in the morning of the wedding day, their fast must begin at midnight before. After Communion, they may breakfast and go later to the church for the wedding ceremony.

When we contemplate the Catholic Church wedding, we must remember that the ceremony can take place in the church or cathedral only when both of the contracting parties are Catholics. Always, where possible, the Catholic Church, looking upon marriage as a holy sacrament, as well as indissoluble, and throwing about it all possible safeguards, requires it to take place in the bride's parish church. In the Catholic Church wedding, the general custom of the processional and other non-religious features of the marriage are similar to those in other churches, and there is the same latitude of choice in the number of attendants, the order of the processional, and many other details of the wedding. The bride's father, however, does not give her away, as in the Protestant marriage ceremony, but retires immediately to his pew as soon as he has escorted her to the chancel steps. The ring ceremony is always used, but the priest blesses the ring before handing it to the groom.

In many Catholic churches — as, for instance, in St. Patrick's Cathedral in New York City — the entire wedding party proceeds up the chancel steps into the sanctuary, the bridesmaids and ushers arranging themselves then in groups on either side, the maid of honor and the best man meeting at the chancel steps and following the bridesmaids; and finally the bride, entering the sanctuary on the left arm of the groom, takes her place with him before the officiating clergyman, who stands on the predella, or highest step of the altar. In some churches, however, the presence of the wedding party in the sanctuary is not allowed, and the ceremony takes place at the chancel steps.

In the recessional, the bridesmaids and ushers sometimes pass down the aisle two by two as in the processional, but just as often a bridesmaid and an usher together. This variation belongs to no particular denomination.

Believing that marriage should be entered into carefully and without undue haste, the Catholic Church requires, in the case of the marriage of two Catholics, that "banns," or proclamation of intent to marry be proclaimed from the respective churches of both the bride and groom to be on three successive holy days — not necessarily three successive Sundays — before the wedding. If one of the contracting parties is a non-Catholic, no "banns" are published.

A Catholic and a Protestant cannot be married in a Catholic church without special permission of the Bishop. Such a wedding usually takes place in the rectory or priest's house; or by special permission of the Bishop, it may be performed in a home, or perhaps a hotel or club. Always, however, a Catholic priest must officiate. Nor does the Catholic Church recognize a civil marriage.

In the case of a Catholic marrying a Protestant, the Bishop of the Diocese is empowered to grant a dispensation for the marriage. Three agreements must be signed by the non-Catholic — no interference with the religious beliefs of the Catholic faith, and that only one ceremony — the Catholic shall be performed, and to bring up their children in the Catholic faith.

There are in reality two kinds of dispensation — one in favor of the Catholic who is to marry an unbaptized non-Catholic, the other, known as the "mixed-religion" dispensation, in favor of the Catholic intending to marry a non-Catholic who has been baptized.

Another safeguard thrown by the Catholic Church around marriage is the requirement that persons unknown to a priest coming to him to be married must present written evidence of their freedom to wed. All must likewise present credentials of baptism. The Catholic Church does not permit re-marriage of divorced persons.

CHAPTER X

The Orthodox Jewish Wedding

THE BEAUTIES of Oriental rites three thousand years old are embodied in the orthodox Jewish wedding of today as it is held in the synagogue. Under a silken canopy, originally typifying the sky, supported by tall standards covered with velvet, their bases perhaps five feet apart, stand the bridal pair, the bride at the right of the groom, both facing the Ark, and the Rabbi facing them and the assembled congregation. The maid of honor is on the right of the bride, the best man at the left of the groom. The other attendants, if any, stand outside the canopy in the usual order.

Upon the "seven blessings" is based the entire ceremony. In itself the ritual is short, taking only seven or eight minutes, but it is often considerably extended by special musical responses, and there is often special wedding music. Beside the minister stands a small white covered table bearing two cups of wine and a small thin glass wrapped in a napkin.

A blessing over the wine begins the ceremony, this, like most of the service, in Hebrew. To the groom the minister hands one of the two cups; the groom sips it and hands it in turn to the bride. Now follows the second blessing and the ceremony of the ring. The Jewish rite does not allow of a diamond, or, in some instances, even a platinum, wedding ring; preferably it should be a plain gold band.

The best man hands the ring to the Rabbi, who, speaking now in English (this is required by the law of New York and many other states), asks of the groom "Dost thou take this woman to be thy wedded wife?", and of the bride the corresponding question. Then he hands the ring to the groom who, placing it on the fourth finger of the bride's right hand, says in Hebrew the beautiful words, "Behold, thou art consecrated to me with this ring according to the law of Moses and Israel." At any time thereafter she may transfer the ring to the usual ring finger of her left hand, for generally it will not slip below the second joint of her right hand finger.

An address to the bride and groom, delivered in English, comes at this point in the ceremony. It is five or six minutes in length; its character varies according to the Rabbi's acquaintanceship with the couple, and other circumstances of the marriage. Following it, there is the "three-fold blessing of the High Priest," ceremonial drinking of the second cup, and the rest of the blessing, all in Hebrew.

Finally comes the ancient rite of the breaking of the glass. It typifies the sacking of the temple in Jerusalem, by ancient law all Jews being admonished in the midst of joyous observances, to remember this tragedy and to hope for the rebuilding of Zion. So the groom, taking the glass from the minister, now sets it on the floor, and crushes it with his heel.

As in all orthodox Jewish religious services, the men guests at a wedding ceremony must retain their head covering. But contrary to the usual custom in a Jewish tabernacle, men and women may sit side by side for the marriage. The wedding procession takes place as in any church, varied according to desire.

If a wedding is to be performed at a home or a hotel in accordance with the orthodox ritual, the nuptial canopy is transported thither, and no other altar is used. If the marriage is followed by a wedding repast, a special nuptial grace is required by the ritual.

CHAPTER XI

Wedding Budgets

How does one achieve a Perfect Wedding with complete serenity for the bride — to say nothing of complete serenity for all the other members of the bridal party? Budget! Budget Time, Budget Energy, Budget Money.

For the average large wedding three months of preparation is the ideal period. True, many weddings are well prepared for — and perfectly — with less time, and I have known successful weddings to be conceived and carried out in a month. "I'm terribly excited," said a bride to me, whose fiancé's plans had made it necessary to set a month hence quite a large and fashionable wedding. "How can we ever do it?" I assured her that we could — and we did!

But it must always be remembered that if little time is allowed for the wedding plans, expenses are likely to be increased; for shopping must be done hurriedly, without time for much comparison of prices; it is less easy to "look around"; there is not time to get estimates and select the best, and get the most economical, caterer or florist, etc. Moreover Our Bride herself must have the fittings of her wedding gown very near the time for the event and they usually leave her tired and strained.

So let us consider that we have the ideal time for the wedding preparations — three months, which provides ample leisure for everything. Our first step will be the making of a "Time Chart." For a Time Chart is the greatest aid to peace of mind ever invented! Work by the calendar from the instant the wedding date is set, and there will be nothing to worry about on the wedding day. (Appendix A)

Our wedding, let us say, is set for June 30th. Our Time Chart therefore will begin on March 30th. Three months to bring everything to a state of perfection that will make this a never-to-be-forgotten occasion.

Two weeks, if possible, just before the wedding — at least one — with practically everything arranged and nothing to do but rest, should be assured Our Bride and all her family. So in this instance we set the last date for the completion of all the necessary arrangements about June 20th, perhaps a little later. Our schedule should be followed as exactly as possible, so that to all intents and purposes Our Bride could really be married on this last day if necessity arose! The last week or ten days, or of course two weeks if possible, is the time for a "let-down" and relaxation; so that all will feel poised and calm on the actual wedding day.

With calendar in hand, Our Bride and her family now block out the two months and a half from March 30th. There are the invitations to consider, the making and checking of the guest list, the ordering of the lingerie, the linen — practically all the wedding plans, even the selection of the clergyman for the ceremony, though the groom pays him. Since styles of clothing change so rapidly, "style shopping" can be left until a little later, and perhaps the making of the wedding gown does not need to begin immediately. But whatever can be done early should be completed and out of the way.

Lists made in the beginning and checked after every shopping expedition are a great saver of time and labor, to say nothing of money.

Planning for a wedding, even a small one, requires the expenditure of a good deal of nervous and physical energy, and shopping is tiring to most people. Never try to do too much in one day, "take things gradually and keep rested" is good advice to Our Bride and all her family.

As each item is purchased, or as each arrangement with caterer, florist or other assistant in the bridal plans is made, it should be entered in an account book. At a glance, then, Our Bride can tell how far she has gone in the spending of her wedding budget, and how much she still has left to use. Nothing is more painful than to have it dawn on you suddenly some day that you have spent too much and your money is almost gone before the wedding arrangements are complete!

Then the Money Budget!

Of course Our Bride and her family, who bear most of the expenses of the wedding, must decide just what can be spent on this all-important occasion. No one, in these days of freedom in wedding plans, need be disturbed because a large sum is not available for the marriage. It is not so much the amount of money spent as how it is expended that determines the loveliness of the wedding. The radiant happiness of the couple, the perfection of detail in the arrangements, no matter how simple, are what make it a success.

An acceptance of what you have to spend and a resolution to make the best of it is the first ingredient of success in this as well as in other fields of effort. Even the girl with a large income often prefers to have her wedding much simpler than the more expensive one her family could afford.

Now let us take a quartet of brides, and consider their typical budget problems. These examples are taken from actual weddings.

JOAN'S $300 BUDGET

Joan is a capable though very young and pretty secretary, and during her year-and-a-half with a large hosiery concern she has managed to save

$200. An older brother, who has a fine job, has presented her with a check for $100. That makes a thrilling total of $300 for her wedding expenditures.

Let us sit down with Joan and see how her wise little head will guide her in making the various necessary items fit into her budget.

Bridal outfit....................................	$ 50.00	16⅔%
Personal trousseau..............................	137.50	45⅚%
Wedding refreshments...........................	25.00	8⅓%
Announcements (150)...........................	37.50	12½%
Household trousseau............................	50.00	16⅔%
	$300.00	100 %

Joan, like some of our other brides, would have liked to be married in her picturesque "school house" church, but even a small country church requires decoration and certain other expenditures; however small, they mount up. So she decided to be married in the informal garden of her mother's home, behind a quaint old-fashioned house. Her guests — the family, and school friends of hers and her fiancé's — she invited informally by personal note (40 in all); she also sent engraved announcements to 150 — those who were not invited to the wedding.

She made another saving on her household linens. She and her husband, at least for the first year of their married life, were to live in a two-room apartment in the city. Her $50, judiciously spent, was quite adequate.

Then came the magic hour — seven o'clock in the evening. In July, even shaded gardens can be very warm; and as Joan said herself, "The shadows from my trees are prettier, the music from my little brook sweeter and the birds more friendly at this hour." . . . She wore a simple white organdy dinner-type dress, ankle length; her head was uncovered to show her reddish-brown hair, made more lovely by the hide-and-seek of evening sunbeams. Her flowers were white and pink phlox from her mother's garden, made into a simple arm bouquet and tied with a white ribbon that, twenty-four years before, had encircled her mother's flowers on *her* wedding day. The one attendant was dressed similarly in sky-blue organdy and carried pink phlox. The groom and his best man wore white linen suits, white shirts, white oxfords, white socks and blue-and-white striped ties; the groom's boutonnière was a spray of white phlox from his bride's bouquet, and the best man's a "bachelor's button."

After the ceremony, in another part of the garden, a simple wedding supper was served — iced fruit cup, assorted cold cuts, a salad of mixed greens, dainty homemade biscuits and delicious homemade strawberry ice cream. With this was served the bride's cake — made and beautifully decorated by her old but very proud "Nanny."

By nine o'clock Joan and her husband bade farewell to their parents and friends, feeling very sad but at the same time exquisitely happy; for they were more than starting a ten-day honeymoon, they were "setting sail on life's sea" together.

AMELIA'S SMALL BUDGET

Amelia is a young business woman who during her two-year engagement has put aside $600 for her marriage expenses. Living at home with her widowed mother, she must make this sum cover every item.

Beatrice has received from her father a check for $1,000. This, he says, must pay all her wedding expenses. He cannot afford an aftermath of bills.

Constance has been in the social whirl since her début. Her family is prominent and has a host of friends. Her father allows her $2,500. He says that he depends upon her good judgment and accuracy to make this sum cover the rather large wedding which the family position demands.

Now let us see how the first of these three brides solves her budget problems.

Bridal outfit...	$100	16⅔%
Trousseau — personal..............................	300	50 %
Wedding refreshments.............................	25	4⅙%
Announcements.....................................	75	12½%
Household trousseau................................	100	16⅔%
	$600	100 %

With a limited budget such as this, Amelia knows that she must, of course, keep the expense of her wedding ceremony to a minimum. By far the greater part of her fund must be used for the bridal outfit and personal trousseau.

How much she would like to be married in a church! In the large city where she lives, the use of the church which she attends, and of which she is not a member, would probably cost her at least $75, and such a sum is too great a drain on her slender resources, besides making necessary other larger expenses. Were she living in a small town, she could probably use her own little church without much expense. Of course the bridal pair *could* go to a rectory to be married. But this does not seem like a real wedding to Amelia.

So she decides to be married at home. A pretty, if extremely simple, home wedding is quite possible even with her small allowance. She decides also upon afternoon because refreshments may be simpler.

Her mother attends to the inviting of the guests, who are to include only relatives and a limited number of intimate friends. To some she telephones. "Adele," she says to one intimate friend of hers, making her call some three weeks previous to the wedding, "Amelia and John King are to be married on June 25th, in our apartment, at half past four. We want you to be here. It will be a strictly family affair. Will you come?"

To others whom she cannot reach by telephone, she writes notes similar to this:

"Dear Mary:
Amelia and John are to be married on Saturday, June 25th, at home, at 4:30. It will of necessity be simple, but I know beautiful. We all hope you will be with us on this day.
Yours affectionately,

Eulalie"

For the many friends and relatives who cannot attend because of absence from the city or because they live too far away, Amelia has wedding announcements engraved. She uses English script, the least expensive type of engraving, so the cost comes within the $75 she has allotted. (*See chapter on announcements.*)

No professional floral decorations are possible, but some of Amelia's friends make a trip to the flower market and procure a profusion of lovely blooms at a ridiculously small price — covered by the few dollars which Amelia saves out of her trousseau allowance, — and her mother and her friends arrange the decorations, massing flowers against the mantel as a background for the ceremony. A friend volunteers to play the piano while the guests are arriving, and she also plays the wedding march as the bridal pair enter from an adjoining room.

Amelia fulfills the desire of her heart by being married in white satin, inexpensive but simple and lovely. It might have been more practical to be married in her going-away costume, but no one would deprive her of the satisfaction of a white satin wedding gown and a veil on this one day in a lifetime! She has had it designed so that it may be her best evening gown later. Her best friend is her attendant. Her husband-to-be has, of course, provided her bouquet.

After the ceremony, and the receiving line over, the guests proceed to a simply decorated table, at one end of which a friend pours tea while at the opposite end another pours coffee; and plates of dainty homemade sandwiches, cakes and simple bon-bons are on the table. The bride's cake forms the centerpiece; though this has been made by a relative, it looks very professional, and is quite the showpiece of the occasion! Pieces of this cake wrapped in tissue paper and white ribbon are presented to each guest.

Amelia's going-away gown is very simple. She is fond of sports, so her trousseau consists of a few simple sports clothes, a spectator sports costume, two evening gowns, two negligees, several sets of fine lingerie, and various accessories to match her gowns. It has taken careful shopping to make all this come within the $300 allotted, but she is quite satisfied with the result.

Her household linen, in order to come within the $100 allowance, of course, strictly speaking, cannot all be linen! But good cotton today is considered quite as satisfactory for sheets and pillow-cases — in fact some people prefer fine cotton to linen — and six sets of sheets and pillow cases are all she has felt it necessary to provide. An aunt has worked monograms on every one — not all brides are so fortunate! Two pairs of winter blankets, two pairs of summer blankets, two comforters, a dozen bath towels, a dozen face towels, a dozen dish towels and a half dozen wash cloths comprise the remainder of her "linen trousseau." All these things, if shopped for carefully, can be bought at extremely moderate prices, and the $100 has been an ample allowance. A shower, thoughtfully arranged by some of her friends, has provided her with dinner and luncheon linen.

Different circumstances, of course, would have altered her budget divisions. She might have spent less on personal trousseau and more on the ceremony proper. Were she planning to live in a hotel after her marriage, the $100 used for the household trousseau might have been expended elsewhere. But considering her circumstances, Amelia feels that she has made the best possible use of her money, and she goes away on her honeymoon quite satisfied with her wedding day, while the guests, leaving, declare to her mother, "How charming everything was!"

BEATRICE'S MEDIUM BUDGET

When Beatrice first contemplates the check her father has given her, it seems like a lot of money! But when she sits down with pencil and paper, thinks of all the friends the family has, and of the wedding she would like to have — doing what her small niece calls "Figgering" — it is quite obvious that the sum has extreme limitations. The various items make her allowance fade so fast! However, she finally reduces the budget to a working basis, making a generous allowance for her personal trousseau, since she is marrying a wealthy man, and cutting down in proportion on other items.

Bridal outfit.....................................	$150	15 %
Trousseau — personal.............................	350	35 %
Going-away costume...............................	125	12½%
Announcements....................................	75	7½%
Wedding breakfast................................	100	10 %
Household trousseau..............................	150	15 %
Gifts to bridesmaids.............................	50	5 %
	$1,000	100 %

Like Amelia, she would prefer to be married in church, but that will entail added expense, and so she, too, decides to be married in her own home. A wealthy relative has offered to provide flowers and greenery from her greenhouses, at which Beatrice heaves a considerable sigh of relief, for floral decorations at a winter wedding, such as she is planning, are no small cost. Now this item can be eliminated altogether.

Beatrice's mother, like Amelia's, writes personal notes or telephones guests; and the wedding announcements are also kept within $75. Half past twelve o'clock is chosen as the time for the wedding, and a caterer agrees to serve a simple wedding breakfast to fifty guests for $100, supplemented by a bride's cake which the family cook proudly bakes.

Then Beatrice, too, wants to be married in veil and white satin gown; and she has four friends whom she simply *must* ask to be bridesmaids. The pastel color scheme which she selects blends very well with the flowers her kind relative has contributed. To each of the bridesmaids, Beatrice gives a charming vanity case; this seems perhaps like extravagance with her small budget; but they are her four best friends and she is going far away to live.

Her household trousseau is much like Amelia's, save that she has also provided two sets of dinner linen, one tablecloth of damask, and the other tablecloth of filet lace. Some of her tactful friends, knowing that she will live in a large house, have given her other dinner linen, towels and such gifts, so her supply is considerably augmented.

Her trousseau, thanks to the elimination of floral expense, can be more elaborate than would otherwise be the case; and with several pretty evening gowns, several sport outfits, all with correct accessories, she feels that it is entirely suitable to the rather active social life she will lead.

Had she been married in her going-away costume instead of in bridal satin, she might have spent the extra money on china, or other necessities of her new home; but she feels very happy to have had the kind of wedding she really wanted, and somehow or other she can manage to meet those household needs later.

Constance's Large Budget

Reception — 200 guests and fees (@ $2.25 per cover and 10% gratuity for service)	$495	19⅘%
Floral decorations — hotel	200	8 %
Music	125	5 %
Invitations and announcements	155	6⅕%
Wedding cake	70	2⅘%
Wedding gown and veil	250	10 %
Going-away costume	150	6 %
Lingerie	150	6 %
Linen	175	7 %

Bridesmaids' gifts, their accessories....................	$130	5⅕%
Personal trousseau.................................	500	20 %
Incidentals — photos, etc..........................	100	4 %
	$2,500	100 %

Constance spends a great deal of thought on the apportionment of her funds, for she must consider the family position, the quantities of friends — and also the fact that the wedding must take place outside their home, since the apartment is too small for such an affair. The sum of $2,500 which she has to spend is not large for the type of wedding, but judiciously used, it will cover a very satisfactory and socially successful event.

A fashionable hotel is therefore chosen for both the wedding ceremony and reception, and 4:30 of an October afternoon is to be the time.

Thus both costumes and floral decorations will be suitable to autumn. She selects a wedding gown of creamy white velvet, with lace cap and tulle veil — a rich and sumptuous costume, which is proportionately costly. She is going on a long wedding trip to South America, so her personal trousseau must be more extensive than it might otherwise be, including a number of evening gowns and several attractive outfits for steamer and airplane travel. In the city where she lives, fortunately, wedding showers are still considered quite "comme il faut," and her friends have supplied her generously with luncheon and dinner linen, so her linen trousseau can be considerably reduced. To her bridesmaids and maid of honor she presents their hats and their slippers, "killing two birds with one stone," so to speak, helping defray their costume expense, and at the same time giving them a generous and friendly remembrance.

The large ballroom of the hotel is used for the wedding ceremony. A curtain of green smilax, hung on one wall, forms the background for the improvised altar, on either side of which are tall floor vases filled with white chrysanthemums. Aisle posts, tied with yellow chrysanthemums, make a path to the altar. The floral decorations cost only $200, a rather small sum for a wedding of this type but judiciously used, quite sufficient. The fifty guests at the ceremony are seated on small gold chairs. The music is provided by an orchestra.

The ceremony over, the wedding party passes into an adjoining small room to receive the guests, while hotel servants remove the improvised altar in the ballroom and set up tables for the seating of a hundred and fifty extra guests invited to the reception. With the facilities of a hotel, this takes only a short time, and the serving of the wedding repast can begin as soon as the guests have greeted the bridal pair. The bride's table has already been arranged in an alcove adjoining the ballroom.

Each of the 200 guests receives a small white monogrammed box containing wedding cake, included in the $70 item for this purpose.

Since the number of announcements to friends and acquaintances of Constance's family, and the family of the groom, is considerable, the sum set aside for this item must, of course, be much larger than in the case of Beatrice's wedding. Naturally only a comparatively few of their many friends can be invited.

Wedding de Luxe

Antique lace veil, $3,000; personal trousseau, $5,000; flowers, $1,500; wedding photographs, $1,000; shoes, $600 — just a few of the items in an actual $25,000 budget for a fashionable wedding in New York not so long ago! Extravagance — I hear you say!

No, I do not agree with you. I know that this particular wedding gave employment and business, in a difficult financial period, to a perfect army of caterers, carpenters, engravers, decorators, florists, seamstresses, waiters, clerks — touching dozens of lines of endeavor. In my opinion, if more of such weddings had been held in the past few years, many a job would have been created or saved, many a business would have been kept from "going under," and many a heart would have been made happier.

Now that I have thus set forth my opinion, perhaps you would like to know where the rest of the money goes in an affair of this kind?

The veil which cost $3,000 was antique paneled rose point lace. All the bride's lingerie was made by hand, trimmed with fine real laces, and monogrammed, and cost $1,500 in addition to the rest of her trousseau. Her wedding gown was $350. Her going-away costume was an original "Paris model," costing $550. Her household linen supply, like her personal trousseau, was $5,000, and antique flat silver in original 18th century design, for her new home, accounted for $3,000.

To facilitate arrangements for the wedding, all of the furniture had to be moved out of the family's huge apartment the day before the wedding, and stored in vans over night. This meant heavy insurance, in addition to moving charges. There were many valuable wedding presents, and their protection required a number of detectives at a considerable sum apiece.

Many guests from out of town were lodged overnight at an exclusive hotel, at the family's expense. A special choir sang at the church. The fourteen-piece orchestra for the reception cost hundreds of dollars.

All other preparations were on the same opulent scale. The bride gave to her bridesmaids gold vanity cases at $85 each. Her luggage was $1,000. And so it went. It was a gorgeous wedding, of course, and it will long be remembered by those who attended.

Of course $25,000 weddings do not happen every day. Quite usual, however, is the wedding costing $10,000 or thereabouts. I think of a garden wedding for which the expenses came to about this amount. A marquee and specially built dance platform on the lawn cost $500. Floral decorations were $600, including some additional embellishment to the garden! The orchestra expense was $400; the bride's trousseau was $2,500. In this instance expenses were still further increased because of distance from the city. The wedding repast totalled $1,000.

But even in a "de luxe wedding," money, by people of good taste, is never spent for mere ostentation. Just as we no longer ever hear of gold boxes for wedding cake, neither do we have gargantuan feasts, bedizened dowagers, bejewelled brides. Rather, large expenditure is put into quality and fineness.

Simplicity and expense are no incongruous terms. Sometimes simplicity actually requires expense. Take a very simple example. If a satin wedding gown is to be made on severe form-fitting lines, it must be fashioned of good quality satin, for the cheaper variety pulls at the seams. If only a few flowers are to be used in the simplest decoration, they cannot be picked up anywhere; for drooping blossoms in small quantities are too conspicuous! They must be of the freshest and finest. And such examples might be multiplied indefinitely.

CHAPTER XII

His Budget

Yes, Our Groom must have a budget too. For though the larger part of the wedding expense devolves upon the bride's family, his expenditures, nevertheless, mount to a considerable figure before the honeymoon is over!

We shall not consider the expenses of courtship, nor the cost of the engagement ring; all those financial problems were solved by him, one way or another, before we entered the discussion. But we are greatly interested in helping him plan his own expenses in connection with the wedding itself.

If the wedding is to be formal, and he has not already a cutaway coat of dark, oxford tone cheviot, he will of course purchase it, with all the accessories. He may feel it necessary also to have a new suit for traveling. Then there is the bachelor dinner, with breakage to be provided for — and probably liquor. There are the ushers' presents and usually their ties, spats and gloves; as we have seen, he provides these if he can, so that they will all be sure to look alike! Whether or not he provides their waistcoats also, depends on his budget allowance.

Our Bride's bouquet is usually no small item; and the corsages for his own mother and the mother of the bride should be the very best! The wedding ring, in spite of its importance, does not cost very much, and the cost of the license is infinitesimal; but he will also fee the minister as much as he can afford. If he wishes to give Our Bride a present, that is one more expense.

And the honeymoon! More of that anon; but it is a considerable item — usually the largest of all.

Now let us put these various possible expenditures into the form of a wedding budget. Remember, though, Prospective Groom, that the budget figured here is an *average* one. Quite a bit of variation is allowable, in accordance with the season of the year and the section of the country in which you are being married. Some of the items can often be entirely eliminated — and no sensible bride will expect you to provide a bridal bouquet far beyond your means, nor an expensive honeymoon trip if your finances are limited.

Groom's Average Budget for a Formal Afternoon Wedding

Cutaway attire, correct accessories	$ 75.00
Bachelor dinner (for 8, including gratuities, flowers, breakage).	25.00
Liquor for same.	50.00

Equipment of 4 ushers and best man (gloves and ties, at $5 apiece)	$25.00
Gifts for 4 ushers and best man	30.00
Flowers for the bride, her mother, the groom's mother; and boutonnières for ushers and best man	30.00
Gift to the bride	25.00
Fee to minister (average)	10.00
Wedding ring, platinum, plain	15.00
Marriage license	2.00
Personal wardrobe (suits, coats, underwear, shoes, socks, pajamas, dressing gown, hat, gloves, handkerchiefs, etc.)	150.00
Total	$437.00

To this must be added the expense of the honeymoon, which depends entirely on where you go and how long it takes. See Chapter XXII.

CHAPTER XIII

Trousseaux

In Bridal Array

OUR Bride today is as sentimental as her grandmother ever was; and to be married in a real bridal gown and veil is usually her dream of a wedding. And why should she not have this desire gratified, whether she has little or much to spend? This One Day in a Lifetime should be hers, to be remembered always.

Now white — if she chose it — used to *be* white. Today it is any number of different things — cream white, egg-shell white, oyster white, ice white, with a greenish tint; or bluish white, or blush white, with flesh tone; or many other "off white" shades. Our Bride chooses whichever one she feels will be most appropriate and becoming.

Nor need she wear white even in a formal wedding gown, if she prefers color. Pastel shades, especially in Madonna blue or blush pink, are lovely for brides, with veils of Madonna blue or blush pink tulle respectively to match the gowns. Or if a wedding is to be very elaborate, gold or silver lamé with veils to harmonize, are magnificent; such a costume, however, requires that all else in the wedding be of equal splendor.

Choice of materials is equally wide. Satin of course reigns supreme for wedding gowns. But there are also mousseline de soie, chiffon, laces in all shades, taffeta for bouffant styles, moiré silk, and varieties of velvet for winter and many novelty materials from time to time as fashion dictates. Organdy is charming for summer even in a formal gown. Materials, of course, should harmonize with the background of a wedding; though satin in a garden wedding may be quite suitable, and organdy in a church.

The style of a wedding gown will, of course, be determined by Our Bride's figure and height. For trimness and grace, nothing is more stunning than close fitting "Form revealing" lines. For a very thin girl, a more bouffant style might be wiser, but a short plump bride needs to watch her lines too! During some seasons, period gowns are the vogue; these usually need considerable attention to detail and should be carefully used. On the other hand, a bit of period detail, such as the high Medici collar of lace, may give a gown distinction and individuality.

The neck of the formal wedding gown, unless for an evening wedding, should never be lower in back than the shoulder line of the neck. In front it may be as décolleté as appropriate; but too low a line is unsuitable to the dignity of the wedding ceremony. In many churches there are strict rules regarding décolleté which must be observed.

With long sleeves Our Bride will not wear gloves. With short sleeves, she will wear long white or pastel gloves matching the tone of her gown, either of kid or French suede. And here let us note a little trouble-and-money-saving device for the easy reception of the wedding ring at the altar! Instead of cutting off the glove finger on the fourth finger of her left hand, making it impossible to wear the gloves again, Our Bride may economically rip the perpendicular seam to within half an inch of the top, and then just slip the glove finger back when the ring is placed on her hand, and replace it again immediately after. A few stitches repair all the damage.

And of course a train must sweep behind her! What is a wedding gown without a train! It may be one yard, or it may be seven yards in length. It may be cut in one with the gown; it may hook on at the waist; it may hook on at the shoulders; and it may even come around the neck and shoulders in mantle fashion. Styles change; and it is wisest to follow the mode.

Naturally a seven yard train belongs in a stately cathedral, not in a small apartment; and a one yard train cannot do much sweeping up a church aisle! So the place of the wedding must be considered in planning the wedding gown.

"Floating clouds of glory" — someone has called the wedding veil. It adds a final touch of etherealness to Our Bride; under it she becomes a being of mystery. Like many other wedding customs, it comes to us from remote antiquity. The ancient Greek bride covered herself with a veil and was crowned with a wreath by her bridesmaid. The Roman bride wore a "flammeum," or bright yellow veil, with shoes to match! In ancient Jewish wedding rites, the bride's veil covered both her face and her body. In mediaeval times among the Anglo-Saxons there was held over bride and groom, as the benediction was pronounced, a square or veil of white cloth, called the "care cloth," partly, it is said, to conceal the bride's blushes.

It must be admitted that the modern bride does not do much blushing, and it is the exception, rather than the rule, for her to cover her face with a veil. Such an arrangement also adds one more detail to remember, for the veil must, of course, be thrown back after the marriage ceremony.

Usually of tulle, the veil may fall from her head to a point six inches or a foot beyond the end of her train. To a short bride, such a veil gives height and stateliness. A very tall bride may choose a cape veil to make her look shorter; or a triple cape effect, the first length coming to the shoulders, the second to the elbows, and the third falling just below the hips.

The veil may be fastened at the back of the head with clusters of orange blossoms (orange blossoms as wedding decorations, by the way, originated in the East, probably among the Saracens, as emblems of fruitfulness in marriage, since orange trees in the East bear ripe fruit and blossoms at the same time). On any kind of a cap clusters of orange blossoms of course may be used to give the finishing touch, or a whole circlet of them, with lilies of the valley, perhaps, sharing the honors.

Fortunate is the bride who has a piece of rare lace in her family, from which the cap of her wedding veil may be fashioned. If there is enough of the lace, it may fall to her shoulders under the tulle of her veil. In style her cap may be of the "Baby Stuart" type, smooth over the head; a coronet effect, to give height, or with a "flange" for the same purpose; or it may be a bonnet to go with a costume of Colonial type; or it may be mediaeval to go with a gown of that period. Jeweled headdresses are not used today.

The hose for the wedding costume should be in flesh tones, not the tone of the gown, for the latter makes the ankles look thick and "Dutchy." Slippers, of satin or crepe usually, should match the tone of the gown exactly. They can be made to order from the same material; or dyed to match the shade exactly. Sometimes a tall bride, — especially if she is taller than the groom, deems it wiser to have the heels of her wedding slippers lowered.

With a simple jewel — and of course her bouquet, of which more hereafter — or a white prayerbook, if she prefers — she is now ready to float in "clouds of glory" to the altar!

THE PERSONAL TROUSSEAU

In olden times, they called it a "Trusse" or bundle — that collection of clothing and belongings which the bride took to her new home on the day of her wedding. Hence the derivation of the word "trousseau."

Whether in olden times the "Trusse" was supposed to provide for the bride's needs for any length of time I do not know, but nowadays it is taken for granted by Our Bride that her trousseau shall relieve her husband of the duty of providing clothing for at least a year! This dictum, however, may be taken "with a grain of salt" when a new husband is well able to provide and she is not!

As a matter of fact, He — quite as much as the amount of money available in the wedding budget for this important item — is the determining factor as to just what the personal trousseau will include and of what character it will be. For it is upon his financial situation, the type of home he can provide, the kind of social life the pair will lead, that the selection of the personal trousseau should depend, and, of course, upon the kind of honeymoon he is able to afford! If Our Bride is going to Europe on a long wedding tour, she will need one kind of trousseau; if she is going to a moun-

Choose Here

YOUR HOUSEHOLD LINENS

When great-grandmother was a bride
Our linens were her joy and pride

NEXT in importance to the wedding-day trousseau itself is the bride's store of Household and Decorative Linens, Sheets, Pillow Cases, Blankets, Bed Spreads and Towels. Some of these may have been ready in your hope-chest, but the greater part of the complete equipment must now be provided.

The Strawbridge & Clothier Store has been famous for all these for more than seventy years — thus contributing to the happiness of four generations of brides! Yes, it is quite possible that your own great-grandmother's Linen Trousseau was bought here.

Through each generation the reputation of our Linens and kindred supplies — for quality, value and lasting satisfaction — has grown stronger. We have far greater variety now than your grandmother ever dreamed of — not only the gleaming damasks and snowy sheetings, but fascinating assortments of inexpensive table linens, bed furnishings and towels with the touches of color that today's brides like so well.

Arrangements may easily be made, if
you so desire, to purchase your home
supplies on our Deferred Payment Plan

STRAWBRIDGE & CLOTHIER
Market, Eighth and Filbert Sts., Philadelphia

tain cabin, she will need another type. If later she is to have her own home, where life will be simple and quiet, her supply of clothing must be in keeping; if she and her husband are to live in a hotel, dine out every night and entertain and be entertained considerably, costumes more elaborate must be included.

Her "going-away costume" might be considered the "pièce de résistance" of her personal trousseau, aside from her wedding gown, of course. It is often made to order, or maybe it is a Paris import. Upon its selection she spends much thought and care. It is usually expensively simple, and as attractive an ensemble as she can find. For how she looks when she leaves on her wedding trip is very important, because that picture, as well as the picture of her in her bridal costume, will linger long in everyone's memory.

Then she will always want one evening gown, no matter how simple her trousseau; two or three are better, and quite often she will need more. Sports costumes are usually necessary. If she is very athletic, playing golf, riding horseback, playing tennis, then her sports costumes should be numerous. If she is like many people who take their own exercise in watching others, she will want the "spectator" variety — and there should always be one or two of this type in any event.

One or two attractive afternoon gowns for tea or bridge should be included. Daytime dresses may be as many as she wishes. All her costumes should have appropriate accessories; she should have plenty of hose; and plenty of attractive lingerie.

But always, as she plans her personal trousseau, Our Bride should constantly bear in mind the financial situation of her husband. If he is a struggling young business man, as he is more often than not these days, her wardrobe should not overwhelm him with its magnificence, making him wonder if he can ever keep her thus adorned through all the years to come! On the other hand, if she has not much to spend on her trousseau, but will later be in a position of affluence, then a few but very well made articles of apparel are her best solution.

Here is a list for the personal trousseau. Some brides may need more; some may need less; but it will form a basis for shopping:

sport coat	spectator sports costumes
town coat	hats and purses (to correspond in quantity
evening wrap	and type with costumes)
fur coat	nightgowns or pajamas
raincoat, rubbers, umbrella	slips
street dresses	brassières
dinner gown	panties
evening gowns	girdles
active sports costumes	silk hose (daytime and evening)

woolen or lisle sports hose
street shoes
evening slippers
sports shoes
negligee
warm robe
mules

bed jacket
handkerchiefs
gloves (street, sport, evening)
wardrobe trunk, suitcases, hat boxes, fitted over-night bag and other luggage as necessary
cosmetics, perfume, etc.

Household Trousseau

Our modern bride is not much concerned with a Hope Chest. The actual collection of her household trousseau does not enter into her charming head or her plans until the date for the wedding is set; then it is just a matter usually of going and buying what she needs. If she lives in a locality where "showers" are the custom, they are most helpful!

Nor does she expect her linen supply to be enough for all the needs of a lifetime. It is merely a beginning; and like her personal trousseau, is not supposed to be an endless store. By the end of a year, "He" will have to do some of the replenishing of such supplies!

The quantity and quality of her household trousseau depend upon many other factors — upon the size of the wedding budget, the future home, the type of life the pair will lead, the amount of entertaining they will do. Even a wealthy bride can hardly hope to stock a large house with everything it needs in the way of such supplies. The city apartment is a simple matter, and the sum needed for its sufficient equipment is really astonishingly small.

As we note in the case of Amelia's budget, the "linen" trousseau is not necessarily all linen at all. Fine cotton or percale for sheets and pillow cases is greatly preferred today by many people to linen, one reason being that linen wrinkles so readily. And the finest of percale is not cheap! In the case of dinner linen, lace dinner cloths are often used instead of the fine damask that our grandmothers preferred, and luncheon cloths and small napkins simplify the whole table linen problem considerably.

We saw what Amelia was able to do with her $100. With a little larger allowance, two or three extra pairs of blankets, two extra comforters, bed pads and washable blanket covers; more face towels, and extra towels for the kitchen might be advisable. Were a bride buying her own luncheon and dinner linen, she might think it wise to provide perhaps four luncheon sets with napkins, two of them specially fine; four dinner sets with tablecloth and napkins of damask, one especially for entertaining; possibly a lace dinner cloth with napkins of fine linen. Also she could add three or four bridge sets; several tray covers; tea cloths and several dozen tea napkins.

Nearly all the markets of the world today are represented in a linen trousseau of any size. Thus there are Italian filet lace tablecloths, and cloths of Italian cut-work; cloths and napkins of Irish linen; and Moravian and Czechoslovakian embroideries. From Sardinia also come fine lace cloths and there are new sheer Italian linens that are very beautiful; while some Spanish linen is popular.

The incredibly low prices of the choicest of these, when you consider their exquisite handwork, is astonishing to the average bride when she comes to do her shopping. So reasonable are they that even the simplest home need not be without beautiful and decorative linens which add grace and charm to every meal.

Here is a list of suggested linen for a "linen" trousseau. From it Our Bride may be able to select what she needs, adding or subtracting according to her needs or budget:

table cloths (dinner)	sheets (linen, percale or fine cotton)
napkins (dinner)	bureau scarves
"best" luncheon set	face towels
everyday luncheon sets	bath towels
tea cloths	guest towels
small napkins (tea and cocktail)	face cloths
lace dinner set ("best")	bath mats
tray cloths	comforters
sideboard scarves	blankets
pillow cases	bed spreads

If Our Bride is at this time furnishing her new home, then another budget would include her house furnishings such as china and kitchen utensils, etc. A shower given by her friends may possibly help her out in the matter of kitchen supplies; china she usually leaves to be considered in the actual furnishings of her home.

THE WEDDING SILVER

The "flat silver," however, is usually provided by her family, at least a minimum supply; and they will usually donate the tea service also, although there is no set rule against a member of "His" family making this gift.

A minimum "flat silver" supply, in order to meet the needs of the simplest household, would include at least:

6 large dinner knives	12 teaspoons
6 medium knives	6 dessert spoons
6 butter knives	12 large soup and serving spoons
8 large dinner forks, 2 for serving	6 after-dinner coffee spoons
18 medium forks for fish, salad and dessert	2 ladles — large and small

A large or "maximum flat silver trousseau" might be as follows:

12 large dinner knives	12 butter knives
18 medium or luncheon knives	18 large dinner forks, some for serving

24 medium luncheon or entrée forks
12 fish or salad forks
12 oyster forks (also used for sliced lemon)
36 teaspoons
12 dessert spoons
18 large soup and serving spoons
12 after-dinner coffee spoons
 3 ladles — large, medium, and small
 4 salt shovels or spoons
 1 salad spoon and fork
12 iced teaspoons

1 carving set for roasts
1 carving set for game
1 fish knife
1 pie knife
1 cheese scoop
1 pair sugar tongs
1 sugar sifter
1 tea strainer
1 pair ice tongs
 Pickle and olive forks (2 prongs)
 Berry spoons

1 ice cream knife

A silver tea service would include, to be complete, a silver tray, a hot water kettle, a teapot, sugar bowl, cream pitcher, chocolate pot. There should also be, if possible, an after dinner coffee service, with coffee pot, sugar bowl and cream pitcher on a silver tray.

To make her "silver trousseau" very complete, Our Bride might also have silver platters, silver vegetable dishes with or without covers, silver candlesticks and silver bon-bon dishes! But she can also get along quite well without them.

CHAPTER XIV

The Bridal Attendants

A s LONG as there have been brides and grooms — which is always of course! — there have probably been friends as attendants and helpers at their marriage, of whatever kind it might be. The warrior in ancient days had the assistance of his friends in carrying off his bride. The Greek bride had her bridesmaids, as did the Roman; and among the ancient Anglo-Saxons we know that the bride was led by a matron, called the "bride's woman," and followed by a company of young maidens called the "bridesmaids." In the wedding party, as in so many other aspects of weddings, we revert to ancient customs.

How many persons there will be in today's wedding party, depends, of course, upon the size of the wedding, the place where it is to be held, and above all, on the preferences of Our Bride and Groom.

BRIDESMAIDS

Of bridesmaids there may be two, four, six, eight or more. However there need not be an even number, and sometimes three bridesmaids, for instance, walking single file, make a most effective picture. Bridesmaids belong to the formal wedding party; if Our Bride is married in afternoon or traveling costume, usually there are none.

The function of bridesmaids is to furnish the colorful background to the bridal picture. They may wear colored costumes or white with colored accessories; materials suited to the season of the year, always hats or some suitable head covering at the daytime wedding, and often some type of headdress at the evening wedding. At a simple informal home wedding, they may dispense with hats. They may carry bouquets, muffs, prayerbooks, garlands, parasols, or gay fans at the wedding ceremony, according to its type.

Their costumes may have certain period details, as may the bride's; they may even wear definitely period gowns, when the season approves of these. All their accessories, should, however, be in perfect harmony; usually their slippers will match their gowns; or if a contrast in color is desired, their slippers, gloves and hats should match. Sometimes each individual emphasizes a particular color, with harmonizing accessories; or all may wear the same color, with accessories in contrasts. Thus for example, if bridesmaids should wear yellow maize, their slippers, hats, and their gloves, if the latter are worn, should be preferably a rich golden brown. Whether they will wear gloves depends upon their costume and the type of wedding. With long sleeves they need not, even at a formal wedding; with short sleeves they should. At a garden wedding, again they may or may not, according to the type of wedding and the type of costume.

Color schemes and types of materials for their costumes are infinite. Each year brings new combinations in color tones. A vivid color display is more effective in a church than in a small hotel room or apartment. The season of the year, the height and coloring of the bridesmaids, help to determine what this color scheme should be.

Let us suppose four bridesmaids wish to wear pastel costumes. They may choose, for example, that two will wear sunset peach and two "Ciel" blue. Or each might be different, — one in yellow, one in green, the third in flesh color, and the fourth in lavender, with accessories either matching or of deeper tones. If they wished more brilliant colors, they might wear, respectively, shades of orange and deep yellow, or American beauty and pine green, or some similar strong color contrast.

Of course colors that harmonize or complement each other should always be placed together. Madonna blue and lavender, for instance, are quite obviously unsuited to close association; but when each is placed next to a complementary color, as Madonna blue beside daffodil yellow, the effect of each is enhanced.

In materials, every season offers new suggestions. Among the most usual for formal weddings are satin, moiré, crepe, velvet, chiffon, both plain and flowered; laces, plain and flowered taffetas, silver or gold metal cloth. At an informal home or garden wedding, dotted mull, organdy, chiffon and similar materials are more suitable than heavy and expensive silks.

And who are asked to be bridesmaids?

Usually intimate friends of Our Bride, though she may ask friends or sisters of the groom if she wishes. It does not matter whether they are married or unmarried. They are invited, usually, as soon as the date of the wedding is set, so as to give them ample time to make their plans. Of course Our Bride makes the decision as to what their costumes will be; their part is to agree graciously with what has been selected, and they generally pay for their own attire. Therefore Our Bride uses discretion; she will not ask girls of moderate means to provide too expensive costumes. From an artistic point of view, especially at a very formal wedding, it may be best for their costumes to be exactly alike; but this is not a necessity. It is optional whether Our Groom pays for the bridesmaids' bouquets, or whether they are included in the floral estimate to the bride's family.

Maid and Matron of Honor

If Our Bride has a married sister, she is the logical matron of honor, and an unmarried sister is the logical maid of honor. But either post may be taken by an intimate friend, or even by a sister or friend of the groom. This is entirely dictated by preference and affection.

There may be two matrons of honor or two maids of honor. This would, of course, be true only in a large wedding. Usually there is one or the other. Maids and matrons of honor furnish their own costumes also; how the expense of their bouquets will be met follows the same rule as in the case of the bridesmaids.

In the wedding procession a maid or matron of honor walks directly in front of the bride, behind the bridesmaids. If there is both a matron and maid of honor, the question of which shall walk first is determined by the bride; usually the maid of honor directly precedes the bride.

It is the duty of the maid of honor, or of the matron of honor, to adjust the bride's veil and train as she turns from the altar for the recessional, and to hold her bouquet whenever necessary during the ceremony. We have seen how she assists in the receiving of the guests at the reception.

The Best Man

There can, of course, be only one! He may be a brother of the groom, a friend, a cousin — or he may be the groom's own father! He is always attired exactly like the groom at a formal wedding, in cutaway of oxford tone cheviot; with the usual correct accessories (see "Costumes at a Glance"); his tie and his boutonnière may be like the groom's or the ushers'; or his tie, his waistcoat and his spats like those of the ushers with the difference in his boutonnière. At an informal garden wedding, he may wear blue coat and white flannel trousers; or, at an informal wedding in house or church, a business suit, but in keeping with the groom always. His duties are manifold; we shall hear more of them in a later chapter; he is the hardest working member of the bridal party!

Ushers

While bridesmaids are more decorative than useful, ushers, we may honestly say, are more useful than decorative. Of them there may be many or none. A church wedding of any size requires a number. A house wedding may need none. A garden wedding may have none; one, two, or more. When there are a number of ushers, one is usually selected as chief usher, and he marshals the others.

One rule is rigid: at a formal wedding ushers should be as alike as peas in their attire in order to give the desired effect of well groomed uniformity. It is easy to see the importance of such uniformity at a church wedding such as we have described. Also the ushers should arrive at the church at least an hour before the time set for the ceremony, so that early guests may be escorted to their seats as graciously as late arrivals. Their duties are by no means over at the church; they are on duty, as we have seen, at the reception also. In the recessional, if it is so decided, each may escort a bridesmaid on his arm. It is not necessary, however, that there should be an equal number of ushers and bridesmaids.

At an informal garden wedding, the ushers may wear blue coats and white flannel trousers, just like the groom and best man.

Flower Girls

Sometimes small sisters of the bride or groom serve as flower girls. They may wear, as in the garden wedding we have attended, quaint Colonial costumes, and carry Colonial bouquets. They may wear simple white or colored party frocks. There may be one or more. They may take the place of bridesmaids at a formal wedding, and if they are from twelve to sixteen, we call them "junior bridesmaids"; or there may be a flower girl or two in addition to bridesmaids and maid of honor. Sometimes it is a pretty touch to have small flower girls scatter rose petals or blossoms before the bride as she advances. Like the bridesmaids, they are very decorative!

Ring Bearer

A tiny little tot, of four, dressed in white or in a pastel shade, carrying carefully a satin cushion on which resposes a ring — usually a dummy one, for he is quite likely to drop it! — is an engaging touch at a wedding ceremony. He usually precedes the bride and her father. If he is very tiny indeed, and there is uncertainty as to whether he may play hide and seek at the altar, he is taken into the front pew as he reaches it; but if he is older and more dependable, he may be allowed to stand beside the best man. A ring bearer may also be a little girl, dressed simply in white. Extremely fancy costumes for children on any occasion, but especially at a wedding, may be aptly described as "gilding a lily!"

Pages

This is a pretty idea, but hardly suited to this democratic country. Moreover, the train of a wedding gown is much prettier sweeping royally down a stair, along the floor, or a carpeted garden path. This idea of pages comes of course from royalty. They are also often used at English country weddings, when the bride's train must be carried over the ground as she goes on foot from the church to her parents' home. Except in similar circumstances, or for an elaborate costume wedding, pages are not necessary here.

CHAPTER XV

A Best Man Tells His Story

THEY tell me that I am a survival of the pagan past — that I am, in fact, a symbolic representation of one of those strong-armed warriors who helped the bridegroom carry off the bride in the long ago days when marriage by capture was the mode! Well, when you stop to consider, times haven't changed so much after all, for if I were not the groom's strong right-hand man through the whole affair, I do not know who was!

It was my first experience as a best man — no, I do not hope it will be the last, though I could do it more easily the next time, knowing the "ropes" now, so to speak; and I have a distinct consciousness of some good work well done. Certainly the day of the wedding was one of the busiest of my life. This was my friend's first marriage and the whole procedure was therefore as new to him as to me. He was quite calm during the period of the wedding preparations.

I had also helped him plan his bachelor dinner, which was a staid affair held a week or so before, and in his toast to the bride, and his remarks on the occasion, he conducted himself with great dignity and calm.

The night before the ceremony at the wedding rehearsal in the church, we repeated many times the march of the wedding procession, and the procedure at the altar, therefore we both felt as if we knew our lesson quite thoroughly.

Jim was anything but fresh and calm when I went to have breakfast with him on his wedding morning. Was it Shakespeare who said, "Fresh as a bridegroom?" I wonder how he ever came to have such an idea? As an old aunt of mine would say, "He was all of a-twitter." Getting married does affect some bridegrooms that way. So I realized that for the day I would probably be his nurse — and I was!

He had mislaid the marriage license — and I found that buried among some papers on his desk. He had forgotten to get a new bill to present to the clergyman, and I attended to that.

Then I had to be an expressman for a while as every best man must be, I saw that his bags were packed for the journey, and that his going away clothes were taken over, along with his baggage, to the bride's house, so that after the reception he would have them there to change. I even went over to the bride's house myself, and saw that his bags and hers for the wedding journey — they were going by motor — were safely stowed in the car that would take them away. I consulted with the bride's mother as to any last minute instructions, and then I hastened back to Jim's apartment. He was a contrast indeed to his wife-to-be, whom I had just found as cool and calm as you please, even after all the rush and detail of the wedding preparations.

It was now time to dress ourselves for the wedding. I had brought my attire to his apartment. Then Jim discovered he had lost his collar button. I could not spare mine of course, and as neither of us had thought to provide an extra one, the matter was serious. It was a wild nightmarish hunt — and still no collar button. Finally I bethought me of a friend in the building and we were saved.

Then Jim could not seem to find his clothes — though they actually lay on his bed before his very eyes — and I had literally to hand him each and every garment. I tied his tie, I adjusted his pin and boutonnière, I handed him his hat, his gloves, his stick — and I practically hoisted him into the car; when he continued to try to put the left glove on the right hand and vice versa — I tenderly sorted them out for him. He had previously given me the wedding ring, which I put carefully in my pocket; and according to a previous agreement, I had a duplicate in a pocket on the other side, in case the ring, passing from hand to hand, were dropped during the ceremony.

We arrived at the church perhaps fifteen minutes before the ceremony, and waited in the vestry. I took his hat and stick around to the sexton in the vestibule. I gave Jim a final inspection, and admonished him to pull himself together. Then as the wedding march began, I steered him through the door and accompanied him to the altar.

Of course there could be no napping for me during the ceremony. As is customary he handed his gloves to me to care for. At the proper time, I produced the ring — and fortunately no one dropped it, so the duplicate was not needed. Most of us rise above our nervousness on important occasions, and so old Jim forgot his and pledged his troth to the loveliest girl in the world with great assurance and firmness. But I watched him with an eagle eye nevertheless, so that if he made a mistake I could set him right unobtrusively; and I heaved a genuine sigh of relief when the bridal couple turned, and I joined them with the maid of honor in the recessional.

But do not think that my duties were over then. By no means. While the wedding party was leaving for the reception at the bride's home, I hastened around to the vestry and presented the clergyman with his fee, and gathered up my own hat, gloves and stick. Then I hurried into a car and around to the bride's house. Strictly speaking, I was also chief-in-staff of the ushers, but I delegated most of that responsibiluty to one I had nominated as head usher, and he attended to the details of their duties. Nevertheless, on reaching the house, I took a general look around to see if they were all on duty; and I checked up also to be sure the bags were safe in the car, and that the chauffeur knew what time to come around to the door. Then I had time to sit down briefly by the side of the bride and partake — all too lightly — of the wedding fare. But I must needs be up and moving shortly to check up on a few final details and I stayed by Jim while he changed into his going away clothes.

Had the bridal pair been going merely to a hotel in town, I should have gone there early on the morning of the wedding, given the rooms a last inspection, perhaps ordered fresh flowers to adorn them, procured the key, and arranged with the management that the couple might go up without registering in the public lobby.

Had they been taking a train, I should have sent their heavy bags to the station, seen to it that hand luggage was put in the car, procured their tickets, given them to the groom as he changed into his going away clothes, or myself put them in his pocket. If they had taken a steamer, I should have had their trunks sent down early that morning or perhaps even the day before; I should have ordered flowers for their stateroom, and again I should have made sure that their car would be ready in time, with their hand luggage safely in it.

As it happened, even in this case, there was a good deal of detail, and after Jim and his lovely bride had run the barrage of confetti, and dashed into their car, I closed the door behind them with a real sigh of relief. Then I rejoined the wedding party for a few carefree dances!

CHAPTER XVI

Gifts

The Bride and Groom Make Gifts

Our groom, in addition to the wedding ring, usually wants to make his bride a present on their wedding day, if he can afford it, though he should not feel obliged to do so. And likewise Our Bride often wants to give Him something by which to remember the day — *he has* been known to forget it when the anniversary comes round!

And both of them, if their wedding is of any size, have their wedding attendants to consider. While brides are not obligated to present gifts to their maid or matron of honor and bridesmaids, it is a gesture they like to make; the same is true of the groom in making gifts to his usher and best man. Such gifts are souvenirs of the occasion and friendly tokens of remembrance.

Our Bride, in making her gift to the groom, usually is limited to a personal article. One rather novel gift, which has a pleasant touch of sentiment, is a plain gold or silver key to their new home. On it might be inscribed in a facsimile of her handwriting, such a sentence as "To John, from Helen, in memory of Our Wedding Day," and the date.

To his bride, Our Groom may give a piece of jewelry, and this she usually wears on her wedding day, as her sole ornament. It may be a string of pearls, if he lets her choose it; brides *have* been known to have quite definite ideas as to the kind of jewelry they prefer!

If he is so fortunate as to possess family heirlooms, Our Groom possibly will have some fine stones reset in modern style, either in a ring, brooch, pendant, or earrings. Or other kinds of gifts may seem more suitable and practical. One groom I know gave his bride a smart town car. Another a cottage in the country. Naturally there is no limit as to the gift when there is no limit as to funds!

Our Groom should always be permitted the honor of paying for his bride's wedding bouquet, for if he cannot present her with flowers on this Day — when should he do it? Often — though this is optional — he pays for the bouquets of the bridesmaids, though naturally he cannot choose them — this would be no task for a mere man! Also, wishing to pay honor to his bride's mother and to his own, he sends each of them a corsage on the day of the wedding, taking care, of course, that the flowers he orders will harmonize with their gowns.

When it comes to their wedding attendants, both Our Bride and Our Groom have a wide choice in gifts, ranging from the merest remembrance to an elaborate and expensive present.

Her own photograph in bridal attire, personally autographed, or perhaps bearing the name of the recipient, in a fascimile of her own handwriting, engraved on a silver or gold frame, is a very suitable present for Our Bride to make to her maid of honor and bridesmaids. She can give them necklaces, bill clips, vanity cases, special perfume, bracelets, folding clocks, monogrammed personal stationery, sport watches or any similar articles within her means, which she feels they may like. Of course the personal touch counts in these just as in the gifts she herself receives; for instance, to give each an article of jewelry adorned with an individual birth stone is a thoughtful selection; and any individual markings signify a personal attention to the gift. The maid or matron of honor may receive gifts similar to those of the bridesmaids, or perhaps a little more expensive and elaborate.

I once knew a bride who gave each of her bridesmaids a sport model automobile, and another who presented early 18th century French gold and crystal perfume bottles. But no one need be disturbed by such opulent examples. The simplest gift is in good taste. They are usually presented at the bridesmaids' luncheon or at the bridal dinner preceding the wedding, but they may be given to the recipients at any time.

Cuff links, silver or gold pencils, bottle openers, combination knife and pencil, leather compact toilet sets, cigarette cases, sport watches, bill clips, dress sets and other similar articles are in equally good taste as the groom's gift to his best man and his ushers. A case of liquor may make glad the heart of each man in the wedding party! The best man's gift need not necessarily be similar to those of the ushers. All such gifts are usually presented at the bachelor dinner.

Gifts to the Wedding Pair

It is strange sometimes how wedding gifts multiply ad infinitum — duplicates, triplicates, quadruplicates, quintuplicates — until Our Bride, to whom they are all addressed, of course, feels her pretty head go round and round! How this varied assortment will ever fit into that new home. . . .

But, fortunately, for the moment, she does not have to solve this question. The all-important He — to whom wedding gifts, incidentally, are *never* addressed — will assist later in making certain important decisions (let's whisper it) — as to what to exchange and what to keep. For the moment it is Our Bride's particular task.

The moment a wedding present enters her home, it should be listed in *The Bride's Gift Record*, which will be found in the back section of this book. The name and address of the donor. The date received; for gifts should be acknowledged within the week received. A description of the gift; this information will prove helpful later when thanking donors, more graciously, by describing their gift, example " — those exquisite creamy white Wedgwood salad plates —". The place the gift was purchased is most useful, when exchange or credit is necessary. The date the gift was acknowledged. Any remarks that may prove helpful from the angles of duplication, exchange or credit, depending on the gift in question. Corresponding numbers should be attached to each gift immediately after recording them. These numbers, in perforated gummed sheets, can be purchased at most stationers.

If possible Our Bride herself immediately writes a personal note of thanks. It should be a real note, full of feeling and gratitude — on as fine notepaper as she can afford. For givers of wedding presents have often spent much time and thought on their selection — it is not their fault that others choose exactly the same thing; and the least she can do is to let them know her appreciation at once.

However, it is entirely conceivable, in the case of a large wedding, where plans have been made within an unusually short time, and many wedding gifts have been received, that it may be advisable and necessary to send the givers some kind of temporary acknowledgment, until Our Bride has time to write a personal note of thanks, and this may even have to be postponed until she is on her honeymoon. So engraved cards of acknowledgment may be sent on receipt of the gifts, the personal note of thanks to follow later. This procedure is perfectly correct and needs no apology. Here is a correct form:

Miss Marie Louise Wood
acknowledges the receipt of your wedding
gift, and will take pleasure in writing
a personal note of appreciation
at an early date

Another form leaves space for the bride-elect to write her name in ink.

SHOWING THE WEDDING GIFTS

To display or not to display? The answer is simple — either display all the wedding gifts or display none!

Of course many a wedding present, ever so carefully chosen by some conscientious soul, is laughable in its unsuitability; and some one Our Bride dearly loves and respects may have execrable taste in pictures or bric-a-brac. But one cannot offend those whose gifts after all may mean more in affection and interest than the offering in flawless taste; and all gifts must be shown together, if at all.

It is quite customary, and entirely correct, to display the wedding gifts on the day of the wedding. Where they are many and valuable, they should be guarded by a private detective — or several. Otherwise a servant or relative should be in charge. To leave valuable gifts unattended is discourteous to the givers, to say the least.

There is no reason why the cards of the givers should not be left on their gifts. It is a gesture of acknowledgment; and it saves time in answering the invariable question, "Who gave you this?"

If gifts are displayed in a home on the wedding day, they are usually shown in a separate room set aside for the purpose. If the wedding is in a hotel or club, the gifts will not be shown there; but they may be exhibited in the home a day or two before, friends being invited and entertained at an informal afternoon tea.

The utmost tact and skill is necessary for the arrangement of wedding gifts for display. Too many duplicate articles should not be put side by side. If a poor engraving has been sent, it should not suffer by too close contrast with pictures of greater artistic excellence. If there are six pottery jars of various colors, they should be spread out to give color and form to the whole display.

But how to deal with this delicate matter of exchange?

"Thank you, Jane, ever so much for those pretty sugar tongs," Our Bride may say, as her friend views the gifts — but perhaps really wondering what she ever *can* do with nine sugar tongs.

Jane, however, is a sensible soul and she has observed that there are eight other gifts similar to hers. In presenting the tongs she has left them unmarked for just such an emergency.

So she nobly comes to the rescue.

"You have several other sugar tongs, Stella," she remarks. "Why don't you exchange the ones I gave you for something else you need? I left them unmarked on purpose, and I couldn't find tongs the same pattern as the rest of your wedding silver, anyway."

And Stella gratefully says, "Why, that's awfully sweet of you, Jane. If you are sure you don't mind, I do need a desk set." And of course Jane is more than glad to provide her friend thus with something she really can use.

Today wedding presents sent already marked bear more often the married initials of the bride, not the initials of her maiden name. The old idea was that everything belonged to her! Today it is the custom to consider that gifts are the joint property of both partners to the marriage. According to English tradition, the coat of arms or family crest is handed down through the male descendant for generations; and marking the silver with the married initial of the pair of course follows the same idea. So children today are not compelled to wonder all through their childhood why mother's maiden name is on the family silver.

As for donors themselves, they can assist the bride a great deal by noting their address on the corner of their card if it is not already so engraved. This relieves the bride of the detail of checking addresses while she is recording her gifts.

When a man and his wife present a gift, their last name should always be used, for it is not always easy to remember who "John and Mary" are, among so many others. In lieu of an engraved card, a handwritten card accompanying the gift is quite correct.

Your Furniture
AND FURNISHINGS

FIVE FLOORS of the great Strawbridge & Clothier Store in Philadelphia are devoted to the furnishing and the expert service that turn a house or apartment, large or small, into the home of your dreams!

Two large floors are filled with Furniture, from the least expensive of reliable quality, to the grades appealing to those without budget limitations. Ramble through our furnished rooms; see the various groupings of classic, period and modern design — almost unlimited variety for living room, dining room and bedroom.

Every bride should visit our HOME PLANNING SHOP on the ninth floor. Here you may plan the furnishing of a room or a home, with assurance of perfect co-ordination of designs, colors, fabrics — a correct blending of every detail in furniture, rugs, draperies, lamps, ornaments. There is no charge for the service of the Home Planning Shop's expert interior decorator.

On the seventh floor is one of this country's greatest Floor Covering departments, and here, too, headquarters for famous Pianos and Radios, and for Pictures and Mirrors. The Upholstery and Drapery and Lamp departments are on the sixth floor, and on the fifth floor the China and Glassware, Homewares and Utilities — refrigerators, washers, ranges, vacuum cleaners, and the innumerable kitchen and laundry supplies.

The purchase of Home Furnishings is
made easier to many home-makers
through our Deferred Payment Plan

STRAWBRIDGE & CLOTHIER
Market, Eighth and Filbert Sts., Philadelphia

CHAPTER XVII

Wedding Feasts

RECEPTION MENUS

WHEN is a breakfast not a breakfast? When it's a wedding breakfast! For the typical wedding breakfast is really a luncheon. It is only at the most informal of early morning weddings that the lowly bacon and eggs are ever "comme il faut."

The "noon wedding" is of course always followed by a wedding "breakfast." If there is sufficient space, guests are usually seated; certainly it is more comfortable to sit down, and it is no more expensive, if a caterer is being employed. If space is not available, the breakfast can be "standing buffet." It should be remembered, however, in arranging for the wedding breakfast, that it is very difficult to handle a knife and fork when standing, and the menu should be planned with this in mind.

Usually, whether guests are seated or not, the bridal party is seated at a specially decorated "bride's table." Sometimes the centerpiece of this is the bride's cake, surrounded by suitable floral decorations. Or the bride's cake may be placed on a small table by itself, especially if the bridal table is in the form of a hollow square or a horseshoe.

Our Bride sits at the right of the Groom; the best man at her right; and the maid or matron of honor at the left of the groom, with bridesmaids and ushers alternately. Sometimes husbands of bridesmaids and wives of ushers are invited to join the party. All are seated by place cards.

At a separate table sit the parents of the bridal pair, the bride's mother having the groom's father on her left; the groom's mother at the right of the bride's father. If the officiating clergyman is present accompanied by his wife, as is frequent, he will sit at the right of the bride's mother and his wife at the right of the bride's father.

THE WEDDING BREAKFAST MENU

Many and delicious are the possible menus for the wedding breakfast. Naturally they vary with the season, having more hot dishes for winter, more cold dishes for summer. Infinite variations are possible. Simplicity is the rule but there may be a certain amount of choice for guests. Ice cream seems to be as usual at weddings as at parties, but it is not obligatory.

Here are two excellent typical menus:

Fresh fruit suprême
Consommé Royale
Rilletes

———

Sweetbreads and mushrooms

———

Endive à la riche

———

Bombe dijonnaise
Friandises

———

Coffee

———————

Coupe carmen
Strained gumbo in cup
Rilletes

———

Broiled spring chicken
New peas à l'étuve
Parisienne potatoes

———

Chiffonade salad
Cheese straws

———

Bombe de marriage

Petits fours   Coffee

The first of these could be easily managed standing; for the second it would be practically necessary to sit down in order to cut the chicken!

For a simpler wedding, the breakfast might consist of hot soup, cold meat and salad, or lamb chops with peas, hot biscuits, and homemade ice cream not necessarily in fancy forms, and coffee. Or another menu might be chicken à la King, bread and butter, salad, coffee, and ice cream and cake.

The buffet table for the wedding breakfast may be covered with a lace or damask cloth or a cloth of embroidered linen or linen with lace insertion. The floral decorations should correspond with those at the wedding ceremony, even when the reception is in a different place. Men guests will usually serve the ladies whom they are escorting; waiters will usually serve unescorted ladies. Behind the table stands a sufficient staff of servants to see that everyone's wants are adequately supplied; or at a more simple wedding, members or friends of the family perform this service. Urns of coffee and tea, and perhaps bouillon, stand on the buffet table, or else on a side table. Guest tables are covered with damask cloths and adorned with flowers.

At the Afternoon Wedding

The menu for the afternoon wedding repast, when it is a real wedding "supper," is very similar to the wedding breakfast. Sometimes a "high tea" is served, which, of course, is a somewhat lighter repast. This afternoon service may be either a standing or seated buffet, according to the size of the wedding. But here again it is much more comfortable for guests to be seated.

A typical and not elaborate "high tea" menu might be:

Bouillon in cups
Rilletes

———

Chicken salad
Assorted sandwiches

———

Individual ice cream in wedding forms

Cakes   Bonbons   Mints

———

Coffee

At a garden outdoor wedding, the following menu was served at small tables under a marquee, and amply provided for the effect of country air upon appetites:

Cold consommé
Choice of lobster or chicken salad
Assorted fancy sandwiches

———

Cold cuts — buffet pieces — (whole cold
salmon in jelly, whole boned capon in jelly)

———

Assorted ices in wedding moulds
Petits fours

———

Champagne   Coffee

The per capita charge for this wedding repast was at that time $3 a cover, including china, linen, silver service, and transportation from the city, with a guarantee of a certain number. The guarantee, as is evident, protects the caterer, who usually bases his price upon it.

At a very simple outdoor country wedding, refreshments might be served from a buffet table by a family servant or members of the family. Such a repast might consist of assorted sandwiches, chicken salad, ice cream, cake and fruit punch. Or there need not be salad at all. The same type of simple refreshments might do very well at a small house wedding.

At the evening wedding, a regular dinner menu might be served, which would always be a seated repast. There could also be a supper served from a buffet table to guests seated or standing, with some such menu as shrimp à la Newburgh, or chicken à la King, cold cuts, salad, fancy sandwiches, ice cream, cake and coffee. Or there might be just simple refreshments, fancy sandwiches, ice cream, cakes, and demitasse.

The Wedding Cake

To each guest at a wedding among the ancient Greeks was given, as he entered, a cake called "sesame," made of sesame seeds pounded, roasted and mixed with honey — the prototype of the modern wedding cake.

So every guest at today's wedding, whether it be large or small, expects a piece of the wedding cake to carry home with him or her — to dream on, if superstitiously inclined! One receives this souvenir possibly in a white box with a silver or gold monogram, tied with white ribbon; or it may be simply wrapped in white tissue paper.

Thimbles, coins and what-nots of various kinds in brides' cakes are largely a thing of the past, though there is no objection to this bit of fun at an intimate wedding, if desired. However, the modern bride's cake has developed a new "wrinkle" to supersede this custom. More often than not, nowadays, the whole cake, save the top layer, is made of white "Lady" cake, instead of the traditional fruit cake; only the smallest and topmost of the graduated layers being of the latter. This layer is encased in tin, frosted with the rest; after the wedding feast this tin box is removed, the icing taken off, and the one layer is put away for the first wedding anniversary.

Caterers' brides' cakes are not prohibitive in expense, and they have a professional appearance quite difficult for the amateur baker to achieve. Still the family cook or Aunt Sophia may turn out a remarkable production that will quite surprise the bride!

A menu card adds a certain amount of éclat to the wedding feast. Naturally it is unsuitable to the simple wedding. But at the large formal reception, when guests are seated, it is decorative and useful. At many hotels, these cards, lettered in gold, are part of the service. In specifying the items on the menu, the high sounding French names which chefs delight to use may be employed or just plain "United States!"

Bachelor Dinner

Theoretically it is Our Groom's last fling in the freedom of bachelorhood. Practically, it is often the staidest of affairs — the Bachelor Dinner to which he invites his ushers and other friends about one week before the wedding. But though there may be a certain amount of carousing, and a good time all round, there is no particular reason why the bachelor dinner should be a debauch, whether held at a hotel, a club, or his own apartment. The guests are invited by word of mouth, by telephone, or by personal note.

Ordinarily there is gay entertainment — perhaps a vaudeville pair, or radio singers, or dancers. The table is gaily decorated; and the groom's presents to his ushers and his best man lie at their places, if he wishes — or he can present them later, if there are guests outside of the wedding party present.

One ceremony is usually an integral part of this dinner — the toast to the bride, accompanied by much shattering of glass, to wit:

At the proper moment, decided by Our Groom, he rises, elevates his glass — preferably filled with champagne! — and declaims, in ringing tones, "A Toast to My Future Wife!" then breaks his glass (by throwing it in a nearby fireplace). Whereupon his guests rise also, drink the toast and likewise destroy their glasses. This custom insures no further drinking from the glasses made sacred by Our Groom's toast.

Bridesmaids likewise are usually fêted before the eventful day. A bridesmaids' luncheon may take place two or three days before the wedding; decorations are more often in pink, a bridesmaids' color. Our Bride has perhaps invited her guests verbally or by her visiting card. Her gifts to the bridesmaids are laid at each place, usually.

Since the rehearsal before a large wedding requires the attendance of the entire bridal party, both at the church and at the place of reception, a dinner for both bridesmaids and ushers in the bride's home or at a hotel is a very natural event, and a simple way of making sure that they all attend the rehearsal! This dinner can be quite informal; the ushers and bridesmaids would be seated alternately as any group of men and women at a dinner; if bridesmaids and ushers have not met before, such an affair increases the congeniality of the wedding party. Or they may be entertained at a buffet supper, if the household staff is limited or there is haste in the wedding preparations.

Sometimes a private view of wedding gifts seems advisable for intimate friends and relatives, and the members of the bridal party; and this can be very nicely provided by an afternoon tea a day or two before the wedding — usually when there is to be no general display of the gifts on the wedding day. Such a tea is informal; and the bride herself usually helps officiate at the exhibition of the gifts; being sure to express her gracious appreciation to any donors who may be present!

ENGAGEMENTS

There is comparatively little "fuss and feathers" about engagement announcements these days. Usually the parents of Our Bride-to-be send an announcement to the papers, after members of the family and intimate friends have been notified, and that answers all purposes.

A party for the bride-elect, however, given by her family on the afternoon or evening before the day of public announcement, is quite usual, her fiancé being among the guests. An announcement luncheon or dinner, while not so usual in larger cities, is perfectly correct if the family desires. At the dinner her fiancé is present; and the announcement may be made by her father or by an elder brother. At a propitious moment toward the end of the dinner, the host will rise and propose a toast to "my daughter, Mary, and her fiancé, James Thorngate," or "to my sister Charlotte and her husband-to-be, John King"; and all will drink the health of the blushing pair!

The luncheon at which an engagement is announced is usually given for the girl friends of the bride-to-be, and the announcement may be made in a variety of ways. The guests may have favors containing the announcement, drawn from a center flower piece with streamers to each place. There are hundreds of other ways to make known the fact of the engagement, in accordance with custom and locality.

Conventionally, the parents of the young man are supposed to call upon their son's fiancée and family within twenty-four hours of the announcement of the engagement, and even though they are in deep mourning, they will make this call. If the groom-elect has no parents, his nearest relatives, sister, an aunt, may perform this courtesy for him. The bride-elect, with her mother, returns the call promptly, within two or three days.

In ancient times the betrothal ring was of iron, a far cry to the dainty and elegant ring of today! Our Bride-to-be may or may not have something to say about her engagement ring. Instead of the traditional diamond (signifying constancy), it may be adorned with some other precious jewel, or even a semi-precious stone. The ring is worn publicly for the first time after the announcement of the engagement is made.

If the parents or relatives of the groom-elect wish to entertain in honor of the engaged couple, they may give a tea, dinner-dance or supper-dance in their home or a hotel. To this are invited friends of the young couple as well as friends of the groom's family to meet the bride-to-be. If no such formal event takes place, or even if it does, the two families will perhaps once or twice, meet at dinner in one or the other's house.

When an engagement is broken, for any reason whatever before wedding invitations have been issued, it is sufficient to insert in the papers a notice similar to the following, and the natural traveling of news from one person to another will do the rest:

"Mr. and Mrs. Joseph Allen announce that the engagement of their daughter Mildred to Mr. Charles Grayson has been broken by mutual consent."

SHOWERS

To the business girl with a modest amount to spend on her wedding, as we have seen in Amelia's case, and to many another bride of small means, the shower is a boon indeed, as well as a pleasant and generous gesture on the part of friends. It may be of linen articles, or kitchen utensils, or dishes — and it is never expected that any gift will be expensive.

To the shower, gifts are brought by the guests in person, and placed on a table; and quite usually the givers insist that the bride-to-be shall open them then and there for all to see! For jollity, fun and a real display of affection, nothing really surpasses the wedding shower, and in its proper place and locality, there is no lovelier or more suitable gesture on the part of friends.

CHAPTER XVIII

Among the Flowers

"FLOWERS are love's truest language," said a New York poet of the last century. How appropriate, therefore, that a profusion of lovely blossoms, the "language of lovers," should adorn the wedding!

Probably there have always been flowers at weddings. The Roman bride wore a chaplet of flowers and herbs on her head. In rural England, in olden times, flowers, mingled with herbs and rushes, were strewn before the bridal pair on their way to the church. Nowadays, no matter how difficult they are to procure, it is always taken for granted that there shall be some flowers at a wedding ceremony.

With flowers produced in huge quantities as they are today, any wedding may have appropriate adornment without prohibitory expense. And the florist, ready to offer his skill and trained sense of the beautiful and suitable, is coming to be taken for granted in the wedding preparations just as much as the seamstress who sews the wedding gown or the caterer who bakes the wedding cake. Not that a family, or friends, cannot arrange beautiful and suitable wedding decorations, particularly for simple home affairs; but in the larger and more formal wedding, the services of a professional florist are almost indispensable.

Do you recall the "set" background of palms we used to see everywhere for every social occasion where floral decoration was required? Funeral, wedding, reception, dance — the palm was always monotonously there!

Those days are no more. New ideas and combinations of shrubbery as well as of flowers are found in this era. The successful florist, like the painter, likes to experiment; his paints are flowers and greenery, combined in new and unusual effect.

To follow the old stereotyped ideas of decoration does not satisfy us nowadays. It is by the creative use of flowers and greens that distinction and beauty are secured in wedding decorations. Such unusual effects add piquancy and charm to the bridal picture.

Thus, for background decoration, "woodwardia trees," whose varying shapes are adapted to different styles of architecture, lovely slender silver birches and delicate dogwood trees in bloom often supplant palms and ferns. Yet palms are ideal if ceilings are very low; graceful and beautiful is the

Cybotium fern, for instance, which falls from a tall tree in graceful cascades, covering walls and ceilings with feathery green.

Such "background decoration" is most important at nearly every wedding. Whether in church, in a hotel or a home, the ceremony should take place against some flowered or foliage background. And some kind of a "receiving bower" likewise requiring "background" treatment, is usually essential at a reception, though strictly speaking, it may not be a real bower as we generally think of the term. Perhaps it is a lattice work covered with smilax, a mantelpiece draped in trailing smilax and banked with roses, or masses of green background broken by tall floor vases filled with long stemmed flowers.

Of course the type of wedding decoration depends upon the color scheme of the bridal party, the season of the year and the place of the ceremony. With these three questions decided, the florist or the amateur decorator is ready to proceed. If the wedding reception and the ceremony are held in different places, the floral decorations in both should follow the same general scheme.

FLOWERS IN THE CHURCH

Simplicity should be the rule in church decorations — especially if the interior is architecturally beautiful. The decorations should then set off the architectural details rather than conceal them. Masses of greenery are usually necessary, in even the small space of a country church; but they should not be so large or luxuriant as to give a gloomy or heavy effect.

The tone of the woodwork or wall and ceiling decoration and the coloring of stained glass windows must of course be considered in selecting the color scheme of floral adornment. In most city churches, the effect of artificial lighting on color effects must be considered. To prepare a church as the stage setting for a wedding is the province of a florist usually, for even an enthusiastic amateur hesitates to attempt such a large undertaking! The choice of greenery, of flowers and of general type of decoration is infinite, of course. Instead of white ribbons, ropes of smilax or even of flowers may be stretched along the aisle as decoration or to restrain the eager guests. Aisle posts may be adorned with blossoms or greenery as an added touch. Occasionally, when a church is too large for a small wedding, a portion of it is screened off to resemble a chapel; this may be very effective but it is somewhat expensive!

FLOWERS IN THE HOME

A home decorated for a wedding should still, as we have already said, be the home that guests know; it should never be so changed by masses of bloom that it can scarcely be recognized. Part of its charm is still to remain the same, and yet be suitably adorned for this great event. Carefully placed and tastefully arranged low bouquets on tables, on mantelpieces, tall bouquets where they are needed, but neither too heavy nor too massive decoration, is the rule for any house.

It is easy to understand that flowers vary in expense with the seasons, and that by using seasonal flowers, grown out of doors, money is saved, as well as a more appropriate setting provided.

The colorings of autumn blossoms offer marvelously beautiful combinations for wedding decorations. Against the greens that are used all the year round, bronze yellow and flame-colored gladioli, dahlias or chrysanthemums are startling and magnificent.

In the winter, however, the most effective decorations, strangely enough, are those that look like Spring! Cedar trees dusted with alum, supposed to simulate snow, and walls covered with white moss may look well enough from a distance, but not near by; and they are a poor background for the wedding ceremony. Soft green branches of hemlock or cypress, with tall bouquets of lilies or snapdragons or white roses, or perhaps these flowers against the soft bluish silver of eucalyptus branches, make a perfect and suitable winter wedding decoration.

"Of course," says a famous florist, "if a bride announced her engagement under a Christmas tree a year ago, and is having her wedding at Christmas this year, she will probably want a Christmas tree at her wedding. And if He asked her to marry him amid the blossoms of the apple orchard, she will, more likely than not, want these at her wedding even if it is the dead of winter — and it is up to us to produce them — and we do!"

The Bridal Table

A bride's table, center of the wedding feast and cynosure of all eyes, should have floral decorations mostly of white, with perhaps a little blush tone or a pastel shade to break the monotony. Variations in these decorations may be obtained from using different types of white flowers, such as a combination of lilies of the valley, bouvardia, jasmine and white sweet peas, with perhaps a few sweetheart roses or sprays of blue delphinium among the white blossoms.

One delightful idea for the bridal table decoration includes large flat centerpieces, while at the front of the table, on the side opposite the bride and groom, a mass of foliage and flowering plants covers the cloth from the floor to the table top. I have also seen a very attractive "umbrella centerpiece" that rises over the heads of the bridal party, but personally I prefer for the bride's table the low decorations so that the bridal pair may be seen.

Guest tables may have more or less the same combination as the bride's table, with perhaps a little more color. Spring flowers in various pastel shades also make an ideal guest table adornment.

FLOWERS AND THE BRIDAL COSTUME

Finishing touch to Our Bride's costume — the bridal bouquet! And so much easier to manage nowadays than in times gone by for, more often than not, it is made on a "cuff" that slips over the arm or hand. This new device adds to the graceful effect.

Like the orange blossoms which fasten her veil, lilies of the valley have always been known as bridal flowers, probably because they come early in the spring and typify the mating time. A still more delicate flower, the orchid, often now supplants or supplements the lilies of the valley; and "spray orchids" make enchanting bouquets. Many combinations are possible — white orchids and lilies of the valley, with jasmine or white velvety pansies or white sweet peas. Nor is the bridal bouquet always entirely white; sometimes the faint color of sweetheart roses is there; or a pale blue tint of delphinium; or the delicate green of the fern.

Tall graceful lilies make a stately and effective bridal bouquet, but only if used in the right setting and by the right person. I am told that the former Mrs. Vernon Castle originated the vogue for lilies as a bridal bouquet when she was dressed as a bride in a stage production, and carried a cluster of lilies. Her photograph was published far and wide — and brides everywhere, tall or short, plump or thin, began to carry bridal bouquets exactly like hers.

Of course Mrs. Castle with her height and stately carriage, could carry such a bouquet beautifully. But a short bride with a bouquet of lilies — dreadful! Moreover such a bouquet requires distance and perspective. When a tall bride descends a staircase, and there is sufficient distance for the guests to have a long view; or when she comes down a long church aisle, then lilies fit into the picture. But rarely are they suitable for a small church or a simple home. The regality of the lily does not lend itself to small spaces, short distances — or short people! And this is only one illustration of the principle that flowers should be selected to suit the personality of the one who carries or wears them.

Married in her traveling costume, Our Bride will wear a corsage; usually she wears this too with an afternoon gown. A Colonial bouquet — that small compact dainty cluster of flowers radiating from a single flower center — is, of course, suitable only with full Colonial costume, or one with decided period details. This bouquet is often modified by a shower effect.

FLOWERS FOR BRIDESMAIDS

Possibilities for bridesmaids' bouquets are as various as the colors of their costumes, and most flowers which may be desired are obtainable whatever the season. However, there is one unusually lovely blossom, the "butterfly orchid," ideally suited to bridesmaids' costumes, which is in season only from the 20th of September to the 10th of November. This, with African daisies, Talisman roses or green orchids, blends beautifully with many types of costume.

Among other flowers suitable for bridesmaids' bouquets are snapdragons, pansies, sweet peas, gladioli, anemones, lilac, mimosa and the many varieties of roses. Pansies and mimosa together are charming; so is mimosa with dark red or yellow roses. Lilac, mignonette and green orchids; lilac and yellow roses; orange flame sweet peas with African daisies and Talisman roses; snapdragons and gladioli are other interesting and beautiful combinations.

But in the case of "all white" for bridesmaids which is very beautiful and unusual too, there are African daisies, white pansies, stephanotis, gardenias, white sweet peas, swansonia, bouvardia, jasmine and many others, which represent as many different "off-white shades" which may be chosen to match white material.

The effect of the floral adornments of the wedding party are as important as any part of the wedding decorations; indeed, the decoration of building or room should merely be a background to the floral effect of the wedding procession.

No matter where a wedding is held today, there are very sure to be flowers. The methods florists have evolved for shipping them are little short of marvelous. Even delicate orchids can be packed in tubes and sent a long distance. As for the time of year — it does not seem to matter at all! They call it "cooperating with nature" — these florists who hasten or retard the growth of plants so that they shall be ready at any specified time. To us who merely buy the blossoms, they seem to have performed miracles!

CHAPTER XIX

Music

A BRIDAL PARTY cannot prance to the altar; neither can it give an imitation of a slow motion picture with feet hesitating in mid-air! So the wedding marches, most important of the wedding music, must be timed correctly; and thus, as we have said before, adequate rehearsals are most important. Naturally the organist of a large church where weddings are often held, or a skilled orchestra leader, is the best criterion for the pace of the wedding procession.

Practically invariable are the two wedding marches — the wedding march from the third act of Lohengrin for the procession; Mendelssohn's for the recessional. Occasionally a bride may prefer some variation in this. The marches from Verdi's Aïda or from The Prophet by Meyerbeer are sometimes used, but they are not considered wholly satisfactory as to rhythm.

It is the incidental music, like the flowers, that helps to create the mystical atmosphere that should surround a wedding ceremony. And always it should be great music, never second rate or semi-popular. In a large church or Cathedral, however, what we might term a "heavier" program is suitable, whereas a different type is more suitable for the small chapel.

Here, for instance, is a wedding music program suggested by the organist of one of the great New York churches: Bach's Choral Prelude, "In Thee Is Gladness"; Caesar Franck's Choral in A Minor; Handel Concerto Number 10; and "Dreams" by Richard Wagner. Such a program would take about half an hour, the usual time for preliminary music at a wedding.

In a chapel, a program might include the following:

> Songs of Brahms or Strauss
> Sonata in A Minor — Borowski
> On Wings of Song — Mendelssohn
> Ave Maria — Schubert

If a choir sings for the ceremony, a suitable anthem is some such composition as "The Lord Is My Shepherd" by Horatio Parker; "Great Jehovah" by Schubert and the usual Hymns. "O for the Wings of a Dove" is beautiful wedding music for solo and chorus.

The church organ may be supplemented by a violin and possibly by a harp, and there may also be a soloist instead of, or in addition to, the choir. Sometimes, at large weddings, an opera singer is engaged. Vocal solo compositions such as "O Promise Me" are sentimental and not in the best of taste. The highest type of vocal music, as well as instrumental, should be used at weddings. However, people are very fond, on such occasions, of hearing familiar songs — "At Dawning" by Cadman, and "I Love You Truly" by Carrie Jacobs-Bond are often requested.

Many large churches make a rule that all music for weddings held in them must be played by the church organist and all vocal or instrumental selections approved by him. This is quite understandable; it provides against "cheap" music in the church, or faulty playing, which reflects on the church's pride in its music.

Sometimes the organist plays softly during the latter part of the ceremony, carrying on through the prayer and final benediction. A quartet can sing "a cappella" at this juncture also, providing a soft chanting accompaniment that is very effective. A good vocal quartet gives a quality of music that, if we are imaginative, may make us think of the angels' singing! A boys' choir, with its fresh young voices, is charming at some types of ceremony.

Suggestions for a quartet or chorus program might include the Wedding Chorus from Lohengrin; or the wedding hymn, "The Voice that Breathed O'er Eden." Sometimes a special poem particularly beloved by bride or groom, may be sung to hymn or special music arranged by the quartet or chorus director.

A simple string trio (two violins and a cello) makes ideal music for a small home, club, or hotel wedding. Harp and violin accompanied by piano or organ are also beautiful; but never — even at the simplest house or garden wedding — unless they are perfectly played! The wail and scrape that an amateur musician on the violin can elicit from his instrument would ruin any wedding.

For a preliminary orchestra program in a church, or at a wedding elsewhere, the following come under the classification of the familiar:

> Evening Star, from Wagner's Tannhäuser
> Liebestraum — Liszt
> Meditation from Thaïs — Massenet
> Ave Maria — Gounod

Other possibilities are "Spring Song" by Mendelssohn, "My Heart at Thy Sweet Voice," from the opera Samson and Delilah, "Serenade" by Drigo, and even the rather hackneyed "Humoresque" by Dvorak is not scorned!

At the reception the orchestra will play a lighter type of music, often of the popular variety. Such a reception program, where the music must be continuous and cheerful, today frequently includes selections from current musical shows. Then when it comes time for dancing, the versatile cellist takes up a saxophone, the player of the harmonium deserts his instrument for the piano. Usually the orchestra will be somewhat screened from the guests. There may even be two orchestras so that the music will not be interrupted.

Whoever has charge of the music for the wedding, whatever the program is, should have his instructions in writing always. This will obviate many an awkward moment afterward.

CHAPTER XX

Special Problems in Wedding Etiquette

THE BRIDE was fifty years old. But she wanted a white satin wedding gown and veil just the same. It had always been her dream to be married in full bridal regalia. And so I helped her plan it. One cannot thwart the dream of a lifetime!

But generally speaking, for the older woman an afternoon gown and hat, or her traveling costume, are much more suitable for whatever kind of wedding it may be — unless, perhaps, she is married in her own home, where she may wear a simple afternoon gown without a hat. As to what age shall be the limit for a gown and veil, that is hard to say. It is obvious that young, fresh faces suit the bridal costume better, but a bride of thirty, by today's standards, is certainly not too old, if she wishes, nor would she be with several years added to her age.

WHEN THE BRIDE IS DIVORCED

A whole new volume of etiquette has been opened regarding the remarriage of divorced persons, and questions relating to the wedding ceremony of children of divorced parents. Many of these regulations are still in a state of flux; and there is considerable variety and considerable latitude in their solution.

For the bride who has been divorced, however, simplicity and informality are generally accepted as the rule for her wedding. She will not wear a white gown and veil, unless for some very special reason, for such a bridal costume still retains its ancient symbolism of virginity. Her marriage will, if it is not celebrated in a registry office, take place perhaps in a chapel, or a church or her own home. In any of the last three places she may wear formal afternoon dress with a hat, and a traveling costume, if it takes place in a registry office. She will have one attendant or none — no children by her first marriage should ever attend her! Some relative, preferably her father, will give her away. While the present-day attitude towards divorce has greatly altered from that of even ten years ago, it is still deemed fitting for divorced persons to solemnize their second venture into the field of matrimony in a very unobtrusive manner. Usually the marriage is so informal that guests are invited verbally or by an informal note.

The parents of a younger divorced bride will send announcements as they would on the occasion of her first marriage, save that they will use her married name without the prefix "Mrs." Thus, for instance, if our friend Marie Louise Wood, who has just married Doctor Martin Gordon Beverley, should divorce him — which heaven forbid, after we married her off so well! — and then remarry, the announcement would read:

Mr. and Mrs. Schuyler Warren Wood
have the honour of announcing
the marriage of their daughter
Marie Louise Wood Beverley . . . etc.

The older divorced woman, having invited her guests more or less informally, will issue her own announcements. In assuming a name after the decree, she, like any divorcée, usually has taken her maiden name and combined it with that of her divorced husband — Mrs. Cornish Barnes, not Mrs. George Barnes, for there might be a second Mrs. George Barnes later and resulting confusion!

Thus, in the announcements of her second marriage, the form will be:

Mrs. Cornish Barnes
and
Mr. Humphrey Ashe
announce their marriage
on Thursday, the eleventh of October
one thousand nine hundred and thirty three
White Plains, New York

Simple decorations and simple refreshments for a few close relatives and intimate friends, is all that this occasion requires. If the ceremony takes place in the afternoon, with the bride in formal afternoon gown and hat, the groom will, of course, wear formal afternoon attire. Naturally if the bride wears traveling costume, he also will wear a business suit, or traveling clothes.

WHEN PARENTS OF A BRIDE ARE DIVORCED

Here again a whole new chapter of etiquette has been opened, and solutions of special problems are very much an individual matter. Generally speaking, we might say, it is sentiment and the bride's sense of what is right

— as well as that of her parents — that will simplify some of the confusion which seems to result. Each situation requires a special analysis and a special solution. Perhaps if we should take a few examples of the problems that arise, we can make this clear.

Suppose a bride whom we shall call Susan has been living with her divorced father, who has been married again. The invitation to the marriage ceremony will be issued by her father; marriage and reception invitations will be in the name of her father and his second wife, since the latter must be the hostess.

If Susan is living with her mother, who is married again, her mother will send out the wedding invitations, and the reception cards will be in the name of her mother and her second husband, since he is the host for this occasion.

But who will give Susan away? Well, it depends. Perhaps she is still in close touch with her own father, as was the case with a recent bride of mine. She felt that she simply must have her own father accompany her to the altar. So he did, remaining until he had formally given her away, then retiring by the side aisle into a rear pew. He did not go to the reception.

Whether a mother or a father will go to the reception of their child when it is being given by the second wife or husband of one or the other as host or hostess, is entirely determined by the situation. Divorce is so casually accepted today by many people, that the presence of one's ex-wife or husband even with the second spouse in attendance, causes no embarrassment whatever; on the other hand, it may be a painful situation which must be avoided. The whole matter must be carefully worked out in advance, so that no feelings will be injured; and the seating at the church will be planned accordingly. There are no set rules.

A WIDOW REMARRIES

A widow may have her own children attend her, if she wishes. With this exception her marriage follows the same rules as that of a divorced woman as to quietness and simplicity. She may or may not have an attendant, just as she desires. She, too, will wear an afternoon frock, usually, and a hat; or her traveling clothes.

If a widow is very young, her parents issue the invitations exactly as to a first wedding, save that her name includes her married name. Thus, Mr. and Mrs. Graham Wentworth will invite guests to the marriage of their daughter "Joan Wentworth Adams." Announcements follow the same rule. An older widow is likely to invite her guests informally; and she and her new husband will usually issue their own announcements. The form she will use is as follows:

Mrs. Graham Brown
and
Mr. George Wellington
announce their marriage
on Thursday, the eleventh of October
one thousand nine hundred and thirty three
White Plains, New York

DOUBLE WEDDINGS

This is just a case, usually, of multiplying by two! There are naturally certain special problems in arrangement which can be solved to a certain extent to suit individual taste.

Let me explain by describing briefly the arrangements for a large fashionable double wedding of two prominent New York girls — sisters.

The brides, one blonde and the other brunette, were attired exactly alike, in Chanel lace gowns on Princess lines, with detachable lace bolero jackets. They both wore plain tulle veils, with "flanges" to increase their height, for they were rather short; and each carried a bouquet of white lilacs.

Each had six bridesmaids. Each bridesmaid wore flowered organdy over pastel slips of a different color, with slippers dyed to match the slips. They all wore small organdy hats and carried bouquets of white sweet peas. There were twelve ushers.

In the wedding procession, all the ushers walked first. Then followed the bridesmaids of the older bride, her maid of honor, and herself on her father's arm. Then came the second six bridesmaids, and the second maid of honor, preceding the younger bride on the arm of her brother. It was a most beautiful and impressive bridal procession. Naturally it required considerable rehearsing beforehand to insure the best arrangement at the altar; as it was, a row of ushers in the rear, and six bridesmaids in front, stood on each side of the bridal pair in a semi-circle. Fortunately the chancel was sufficiently large for this arrangement. The recessional was the reverse of the procession, save, of course, that the brides and grooms walked together in pairs.

Now it would have been perfectly correct — and would really have been preferred by these sisters — for them both to go to the altar escorted by their father, one on each arm. But the aisle was not wide enough for this. Had they done so, however, all the bridesmaids would have walked together, arranged so that the colors of their costumes would harmonize. If two brides in a double wedding are friends instead of sisters, it is always necessary for each to walk with her own escort and wedding attendants.

It is not necessary, in a double wedding, for the brides to be dressed alike or for their respective groups of attendants to wear the same type of costume, as long as there is general harmony. And there may be many wedding attendants or none. A perfectly informal double wedding — with two brides in afternoon costume and no attendants — is very charming. There is something about two sweet young creatures being married at the same ceremony that is doubly moving!

Invitations for a formal double wedding follow the same general form as invitations for any wedding, save that there are two sets of names. The father and mother issuing the invitations would of course say "the marriage ceremony of their daughters" or a brother would say "the marriage ceremony of his sisters."

To make this perfectly clear, let us set the form down exactly as it would be if Marie Louise Wood and her sister had been married at the same time:

Mr. and Mrs. Schuyler Warren Wood
request the honour of your presence
at the marriage ceremony of their daughters
Marie Louise

to

Doctor Martin Gordon Beverley

and

Margaret Ellen

to

Mr. Angus Ogilvie
on Thursday, the tenth of June
at half after four o'clock
Saint Giles Cathedral
New York

THE MILITARY WEDDING

The procedure at a military wedding, so far as the ceremony proper goes, does not differ from that at any other formal wedding. When the ushers are in army service, as is usual on such occasions, they will wear their full dress uniforms, with sabres. And at the close of the ceremony, as the bride and groom — the groom also in full dress uniform — come out of the church or wherever the ceremony is held, the arch of sabres held over their heads by the ushers is the special feature that marks this type of wedding. The arch of sabres, incidentally, is a very old custom, originated by the British and the Dutch.

Indeed, the military wedding is most impressive and colorful. The "full dress" uniform worn by officers on such occasions is a single breasted dark blue coat with two rows of gold buttons; and a standing collar with black braid on the edge; trousers are lighter blue, with a stripe denoting the branch of the service; and "side arms" with the sabre are worn. Further information about the details of military weddings is easily available from the Adjutant General of the War Department in Washington, D. C., and naval wedding procedure, which is similar, with swords used instead of sabres, can be obtained from the same source.

CHAPTER XXI

How to Meet Emergencies

ABOUT a charmingly appointed table sat a bridal party, the bride lovely in satin wedding gown and veil; the bridesmaids and maid of honor gay in pastel costumes; the groom, the best man and ushers in formal attire for an afternoon wedding. There were quips and laughter; the gay bantering and jollity that attends any wedding, large or small.

Then as the repast drew to a close, the groom arose and raised his glass. The other members of the party arose also and stood in silent expectancy.

"To a beloved bride who is gone," said the groom reverently, and they drank a solemn toast. The bride's eyes filled with tears.

For the "beloved bride" was her own mother, who a few short weeks before, with wedding plans completely made and the invitations issued, had suddenly passed away. But at the very last, she had called her daughter to her side, and exacted her promise to hold the wedding exactly as she had planned. So the daughter was wed in white gown and veil, in accordance with her mother's wish, attended by her bridesmaids, and surrounded and comforted by near relatives and friends. No invitations were recalled, since it had been planned as a small wedding anyway. To hold it thus was an unusual procedure — but quite correct in view of the circumstances.

"Man proposes — God disposes" in wedding plans as in all of life, and divers are the emergencies that necessitate sudden changes in the wedding picture. The illness or decease of a member of one of the immediate families, the untimely illness of the bride or groom, an accident, a financial failure — any one of a dozen happenings may interfere with the carrying out of the wedding as planned. A bride *has* even been known to change her mind while the guests were waiting at the church, though fortunately this happens but seldom!

Suppose a parent of Our Bride or Groom suddenly passes away a week or so before the wedding, after most of the acceptances have been received and the wedding gifts have arrived. Under such circumstances, naturally, the wedding is likely to be indefinitely postponed.

So every guest who has accepted is immediately notified by note, telephone or telegram, according to the distance. Notices of the postponement or cancellation are sent to the newspapers. Such a notice will run approximately as follows:

"Owing to the sudden death of Mrs. Schuyler Warren Wood, the marriage of her daughter, Marie Louise Wood, to Doctor Martin Gordon Beverley has been indefinitely postponed."

If there is time, engraved cards may be prepared, bearing substantially the same wording.

It is entirely possible, for various reasons, such as Our Groom sailing to take a position abroad, or some other event impossible to postpone, that the wedding may have to take place just the same. But it will then be very quiet and very informal. Our Bride will probably choose to be married in her traveling costume, and only close relatives will attend. Just what shall be done in a case of this kind will be entirely determined by sentiment and feeling and by the circumstances.

Now suppose Our Bride to be taken suddenly ill the day before a large wedding. Then naturally the wedding must be postponed, and as in the case of a death in the family, telephone and telegraph employed to notify the guests. In this case it is of course assumed that the ceremony will take place when she recovers, but if she has been very ill very likely it will not be carried out in the same large way. Eventually the pair will probably be married quietly at home with only the members of the immediate families present.

If in the case of a death in the family, and the wedding actually takes place, either on the date set, in a less formal way, or on a later date, within a moderate period after postponement (a maximum of three months), the wedding gifts need not be returned. But if the wedding is "indefinitely postponed" it is usually considered to be automatically "off" and then the gifts must be sent back to the donors.

The illness or even sudden death of a bridesmaid or usher is, of course, upsetting to wedding plans, but unless this person is a member of one of the immediate families, such a happening need not materially alter the plans for the wedding. If there is sufficient time, the vacant place may be filled — usually easier in the case of an usher than in the case of a bridesmaid, because of costume requirements. If there is not time for substitution, there is merely a vacant place, or a rearrangement of the bridal party. Here again sentiment must decide.

In dealing with any wedding emergency involving illness or death, circumstances and sentiment must both be considered. While the decease of any immediate member of the family who is in the vicinity usually causes the cancellation or alteration of elaborate wedding plans, it is quite conceivable, for instance, that the death of a brother of the bride living in another part of the country and not expected at the wedding, would not, for example, be considered sufficient cause for any change. On the other hand, the demise of a dear aunt living with the family might affect the plans much like the death of a parent. Also, if a parent were seriously ill, and there were reasons why the wedding must take place on the date planned, it could even be performed at the bedside of the sick person, providing he or she wished.

In the case of illness causing a change in wedding plans, if time permits, a card similar to the following may be issued to the guests:

Mr. and Mrs. Schuyler Warren Wood
regret that, owing to illness in the family
the invitation to
their daughter's wedding
on Thursday the 10th of June
must be recalled

When an engagement is broken off for any reason after wedding invitations have been issued, an engraved form like the following may properly be used:

Mr. and Mrs. Schuyler Warren Wood
announce that the marriage of their daughter
Marie Louise
to
Doctor Martin Gordon Beverley
will not take place

Announcements sent to the society pages of the newspapers should read: "The engagement of Miss Marie Louise Wood to Doctor Martin Gordon Beverley has been broken by mutual consent."

CHAPTER XXII

Honeymoons

And now your honeymoon begins. The hectic days of preparation are over and the focal point of it all — the wedding itself — has become your most treasured memory. Now, for a brief enchanted interlude, two of you will live in a world of your own, done with the past and not quite ready for the future. You're on your honeymoon.

Where are you going? Well, there's a whole planet to choose from. Two things will restrict you: time and money. Yet you needn't have so much of either. It depends mainly on your tastes — yours and his.

Let's say the two of you are talking the matter over. While the honeymoon is entirely the groom's expense and responsibility, too often he will try to leave most of the selecting and figuring to you. Don't let him. That's the *first* thing you'll have to agree on.

The next is where to go. Knowing how long you can take and how much you have to spend, perhaps you can get an idea from the rest of this chapter. I've listed representative places to honeymoon in roughly increasing order of expense. Your own travel agent, naturally, is the man to see about details.

But before you set your hearts on some particularly appealing spot, there are certain things to keep in mind. Travel can be stimulating and enjoyable — or it can be tiresome and irritating. You must take care of everything you can in advance. Let's consider a few —

PRELIMINARY POINTERS

The various aspects of a honeymoon add up. Travel costs money for more than just transportation. There are living expenses. New luggage. Clothes. Tips. Things to buy wherever you are. All manner of incidentals.

If your honeymoon is to be spent inside U. S. borders, you will probably be driving or taking a train. Remember food and lodging if you drive. Railroad diners are not cheap. Figure such costs ahead of time. If you're lucky enough to be honeymooning on a cruise ship or a trip to foreign shores, you must figure in transportation for two from your home town to New York or San Francisco and back. Things like that are easy to overlook.

You will know about your luggage requirements as soon as your destination is settled. Where you go determines what you wear, and that plus your length of stay decides how much luggage you must carry. With the average resort or cruise wardrobe the bride and groom can travel up to three weeks on two bags apiece, plus a hatbox for her. Beyond that you should really pool your belongings in a lightweight trunk and take small extra bags only for toilet articles and light, frequently-worn clothing. Sports equipment, such as golf bags, will add to the total number of pieces.

As to clothes — it depends on where you go and at what season of the year. Generally speaking, honeymooners seem to prefer moderate climates — cool in Summer and warm in Winter. On that basis you can plan to dress about as you would at home in Summer. Light dresses, spectator sports outfits for the bride; tropical worsted or linen suits for the groom. Remember a wrap for unexpectedly cool nights — particularly in Winter!

The exception to this, of course, is if you are going to colder country for Winter sports. Only a minority of honeymooners do, and they must already be familiar with clothing needs in such climates.

Formal clothes will be necessary in the larger, dressier hotels and, with certain qualifications, aboard ship. Most people dress for dinner en route to Bermuda or Nassau or Europe. Most people do *not* dress on West Indies cruises. Going to Europe, it's partly governed by the size of the boat and partly by where you are seated at table. On most boats it is really up to the individual, and much more customary in First Class than in Tourist.

Since even the biggest trunk is a poor substitute for your closet at home, choose your honeymoon wardrobe with an eye to making one outfit serve the purpose of two. Adroit use of accessories will keep one simple costume looking like half-a-dozen. However, if you're going out of the United States don't forget to take along *plenty of personal linen*. You can't rely on laundries and dry cleaners for either safe or reasonable work.

Another point about packing your bags too full: wherever you go, there will be things to buy and bring back with you. Allow room for them!

Before you start off, the only thing to say about incidental expenses is that they do crop up. Tipping is a universal evil, and must be allowed for. Aboard ship, figure approximately 5 to 10% of the cost of your tickets. Thus if your passage to Europe is $200 apiece, one way, each of you will give about $5 to your table steward and $2 to his assistant, $5 to your cabin steward (or stewardess, if you make use of her services), a dollar or two to the deck steward, another dollar to the "boots" who cleans your shoes each night, and as much to the bar steward as you would in any bar at home. All tips are distributed the last day of the voyage, though you may tip the bar steward as he serves you, if you prefer. On longer voyages tip proportionately.

Besides tips, there are passport visas if you're going abroad; the government tax collected in places like Bermuda, where no passport is required; taxis, always nipping into your pocketbook when you least expect them;

extra films for your camera; in fact, all the little items that don't appear in the major sections of your budget devoted to "Transportation," "Room and Board," and so on. The little items can make a big total.

Now for specific honeymoon spots. I've taken three general categories — American resorts; nearby foreign resorts and short cruises; more distant lands and longer cruises. But here's a tip — if you're looking for a honeymoon out of the ordinary, one that doesn't necessarily involve a trek into the jungle or a canoe trip down the Volga — try some well-known resort out of season. There are few visitors then and prices are at rock-bottom. Try it if you're looking for solitude rather than crowds. It may surprise you.

At any rate, here we start off with —

American Resorts

There is so much to see in this great land of ours that I find it hard to attempt even a partial coverage of honeymoon possibilities. But surely you'll want to travel outside of your own section of the country. With that idea in mind, let's consider the United States in four general divisions — East, Middle-West, South and Far West.

Each section, naturally, offers its own attractions. And the time of year will have much to do with where you go. With the already mentioned exception of Winter-sports enthusiasts, most honeymooners want to go South or West in the Winter and Spring. In the Summer it doesn't seem to matter much, so long as they avoid heat and arrange to take advantage of scenic delights. The Fall is a special season when no one tide of travel is well-defined and people tend to go wherever their fancy moves them.

Motoring is not pleasant in most areas before March or after October, but the trains always run and the airlines can be relied upon except when the weather is simply impossible. When you get where you are going, you can always hire a car by the day or week. And while we're on the subject of money, you can figure an average of $10 per day per person, with meals, at practically all of America's better resort hotels. Some go higher in certain months — but your travel agent can keep you informed on developments like that.

The East

This includes the heavily-populated, industrial part of the country, as far south as Virginia and as far west as Ohio. You wouldn't choose many places here for a honeymoon. The main exception is New England, which is hard to beat when Summer comes. The ocean keeps the coast cool (and makes the swimming the same way at most places). Cape Cod, the southeastern corner of Massachusetts, is charming in both atmosphere and climate. North of

Boston lies Maine, a Summer paradise for those who like sailing, canoeing, hiking and other such vigorous outdoor activities. Bar Harbor, small and exclusive, is the center of social life.

Two other New England states which draw swarms of Summer visitors are Vermont and New Hampshire. Each has many lakes — and, inevitably, quantities of Summer camps. But there are also quiet hotels, lovely mountain scenery, clear sunny days and plenty to do if you're in the mood. Perhaps the best way of all to honeymoon in New England is by taking a motor trip.

Incidentally, the hills of Vermont and New Hampshire are almost always snow-covered in Winter. Wonderful skiing, snowshoeing and the like. The same is also true (provided the weather stays cold) in northern New York state.

The Middle-West

Like the East, there is little for honeymooners in the great agricultural and manufacturing area which runs from Ohio across through Kansas, Nebraska and the Dakotas. Even a motor trip is likely to be monotonous unless you're making a survey of industrial conditions in America. Which seems hardly probable.

However, the Middle-West also has its exception to the rule — this time the region near the Canadian border. The northern peninsula of Michigan, especially, is like New England in that it attracts droves of city dwellers on their Summer vacations. Northern Wisconsin and Minnesota are about the same. In all three states the emphasis is on informal outdoor life, but little attempt is made to cater to honeymooners as such.

The South

From Virginia down and across through Texas, life moves at an easier pace than in the urban North. People aren't packed so closely together. There is more natural beauty and more space to enjoy it in. Motoring through the South — with or without a specific destination — is a real experience. The mountains of Virginia, West Virginia and Tennessee are gorgeous, particularly in the Spring. In fact, there is much more to see in this region than could possible be listed in this limited space.

If you're looking for a resort at which to spend two or three carefree weeks, I suggest trying Virginia or West Virginia in the Spring or Fall. Both states are rich in history and scenic loveliness. At White Sulphur, West Virginia, the Greenbrier Hotel and Cottages is one of the loveliest honeymoon places we can recommend. Greenbrier Hotel has been a favorite with honeymooners since Southern society really *was* Southern society. A romantic,

Then AND NOW...
A GLAMOROUS WEDDING TRIP

• For the past Century, The Greenbrier has been inseparably linked with honeymoon plans. Generation after generation of brides and grooms have chosen America's Most Beautiful All-Year Resort — until now it's the traditional wedding trip.

• Today, White Sulphur Springs is as glamorous as ever. You'll find no more romantic spot in the world — or finer facilities. Here are golf, tennis, skeet, swimming and riding at their best!

The story of The Greenbrier — told in pictures — will gladly be sent to you upon request.

The Greenbrier Hotel
AND COTTAGES • L. R. JOHNSTON • GENERAL MANAGER

WHITE SULPHUR SPRINGS • WEST VIRGINIA

truly lovely spot, with every kind of outdoor activity. It is open all year. If you want to know more about Greenbrier write to them and mention Wedding Embassy and I am sure you will get very special attention. Virginia is also delightful along the coast in Summer, but beware the Winter there — it won't be as warm as you might hope.

Farther south the thermometer rises and we find a real Winter playground region. This starts in the Carolinas, goes down through Georgia to Florida and then runs west along the Gulf of Mexico to New Orleans. You would never visit most of this section in Summer. But Spring and Fall are lovely in the Carolinas, and Florida is a state that "has everything" for Winter visitors.

In fact, Florida deserves special mention. With this marvelous Winter climate it naturally brings people from all over the country. Perhaps you don't want such a crush around you — but you can dodge most of it by not going to Miami. There are splendid hotels dotted along both the east and west coasts, and activities include swimming, tennis, golf, horse-racing, deep-sea fishing, just plain loafing — or what have you? Note that the east coast is gay — Miami, Palm Beach and Daytona set the pace — while the west or Gulf coast is a bit on the quiet side — as in Tampa and Sarasota.

The same lazy Gulf atmosphere continues over into Mississippi and Louisiana, in both of which you may find ideal honeymoon spots if you go in early Spring. Ask your travel agent.

The Far West

This tremendous chunk of territory includes mountains, deserts, lakes, rivers, plateaus, canyons — and California. It's an area to see by rail or motor for its purely visual value. It's so big that I could never detail its varied and various attractions.

You know that in Summer the Colorado mountains have a great appeal. So has the dude ranch country in Wyoming and Montana. Ever consider a dude ranch honeymoon? It will cost around $60 per week per person, but that price includes *everything* and guarantees you your fill of healthy outdoor life. In the Winter you can get the same thing in Arizona, when snow and cold have chased visitors away from the northern Rockies. At the same time the snow and cold give all its charm to a famous Idaho resort — Sun Valley.

If you don't want a dude ranch or a stay in the Rockies, try a leisurely motor tour of some of the National Parks. They're splashed all over the West, providing scenery and education at one fell swoop. Everywhere you'll find comfortable hotels. Everywhere you'll see sights worth writing home about.

But if it's sights you're after, perhaps California is the answer. Like Florida, this state "has everything." It runs the gamut from poised and metropolitan San Francisco to sprawled and fascinating Los Angeles. In between are the country's highest mountains, desert resorts like Palm Springs, Winter playgrounds in the high Sierras, fashionable Santa Barbara and Del Monte, the endless blue Pacific — take your pick. Generally speaking, the southern part of the state is best in Winter and the northern part in Summer. But California has so much to offer that you'd honestly better go see it for yourself.

North of California, Oregon and Washington also present much to lure the passing visitor or the honeymooning couple who want to "stay awhile." Both states are warm along the coast the year round. Both have high mountains well suited for Winter sports. They're like the rest of the West — it's much more enjoyable to see them than to read about them.

Nearby Foreign Resorts and Short Cruises

If your budget allows it, very possibly you want to get away from the United States for your honeymoon. After all, the chance may not come again soon. Take advantage of it if you can!

Nearby attractions outside our borders include Canada and Mexico, of course — also the tiny islands dotted along the Atlantic coast, and the American-owned but foreign-seeming islands of Hawaii. There are many cruises out of New York that serve all these places except Hawaii. But cruises vary with the season and your travel agent can tell you all about them.

Let's just take a quick look at some nearby honeymoon possibilities.

Canada

The great British dominion to the north of us is foreign soil — but still enough like the United States to make you feel instantly at home. Go in Spring, Summer or Fall to see the country by rail or motor — that is, the southern section. The greater part of Canada is impassable except by canoe or on horseback, and in Winter only a small area in the eastern provinces is open to visitors. But that small area provides some of the best Winter sports in North America.

In warmer weather the country's attractions range from famed Gaspe, the peninsula east of Quebec where French-speaking peasants still live the life of old France, to the Canadian Rockies, grander even than our own. The latter are so huge that you can go in only by railroads (though highways are slowly being built). Once there, however, you have Banff and Lake Louise and Jasper National Park and — well, some of the most gorgeous scenery in the world.

Mexico

Not to be recommended to the comfort-loving honeymooner, Mexico offers sheer fascination to those who will take the trouble to look for it. New sights, new sounds, new interests are there. A social system centuries old is in the throes of transition. The native life is as colorful and bewildering as the land itself. Try Mexico if you want something different — at almost any season.

Railroads are still the best way to get about, but highways are being pushed to completion and there is excellent air service. You will probably make your headquarters at Mexico City and set out to see the country from there. What will you see? Ask your travel agent.

Bermuda

What attracts so many visitors? Well, you have heard a great deal about Bermuda, and whatever you have heard probably is not enough. One factor is convenience, of course. The Furness Bermuda boats sail on an average of twice a week and round trip fare is as low as $60 per person; the trip takes forty hours, meaning a day and two nights. On the great luxurious sky-liners of Pan-American and Imperial Airways, round trip fare is $120 per person; it's a five-hour hop from New York in Summer and from Baltimore in Winter. You can also go from Baltimore in Summer, via New York. All of which is to say that Bermuda is both simple and pleasant to get to.

What do you find when you arrive there? A lovely tranquil island, its pink coral beaches and deep blue water smiling at the sun; never an automobile, only bicycles spinning along shady white roads and buggies clop-clopping down the streets of Hamilton, Bermuda's diminutive capital. The real season is from December to April but it can be truly called an all the year island. Bathing, fishing, tennis, golf, exploring, dancing and shopping for lovely English gadgets. The Belmont Manor and The Inverurie are among its most recommendable hotels, charming and selective and yet their rates are kind to the budgets of newlyweds. Write to their New York office, Bermuda Hotels, 500 Fifth Avenue, New York, or to us and we gladly will send you more information about them.

Nassau

Nassau, capital of the Bahama Islands, is more cosmopolitan and perhaps more expensive. Deep-sea fishing is a major pastime. Here, there is a distinct season running from December through April.

West Indian Islands

I wouldn't suggest Cuba for a honeymoon. It makes a lovely stopping-off place in a longer trip, but the island is too busy with its own affairs to provide much for an extended visit.

Jamaica is something else. British-owned like Bermuda and the Bahamas, it is much farther south and consequently even more placid to the eye. It is very mountainous, which means a complete climatic range from seashore to 7,000 feet. There is plenty to do in Jamaica, centering around the British colonial capital of Kingston. Montego Bay is known as a fashionable resort. It is a thrilling place and it will cast a most wonderful spell over you. If you want to know more about it write to us.

Puerto Rico, our own West Indian island, is full of Puerto Ricans. That makes it fun to look at in passing, but perhaps a little crowded for a full honeymoon. Also American are the Virgin Islands, whence comes a fine grade of rum. Other islands stretch away to the east and south in a long string — Martinique, Barbados and many more. They're best seen from the deck of a cruise ship.

Hawaii

The only remaining nearby "foreign" resort is, of course, the Territory of Hawaii. There native culture meets and blends with Chinese, Spanish, Portuguese, Japanese, Polynesian — and the whole lives amicably under American rule. Thus "The Islands" are a place of confusion, turmoil — and peace.

It shouldn't be necessary for me to detail the many charms of this North Pacific paradise. You know about its palm trees and pineapples, sugar cane and beach boys, surfboards and volcanoes. And it knows virtually no season. By ship from Los Angeles or San Francisco you can go to Hawaii for a glorious honeymoon at any time of year.

Which brings us to a longer trip that is the embodiment of every romantic dream you have ever had. It takes a fairly large budget. But it fulfils the hope of visiting the Orient — something few honeymooners want to do under present conditions. Let's consider —

MORE DISTANT LANDS AND LONGER CRUISES
South Seas Cruises

To Hawaii, Samoa, Fiji, New Zealand, Australia. Magic names, those. You can turn them into living experiences on a trip taking about seven weeks from San Francisco or Los Angeles.

This is a cruise to treasure. It touches at primitive, tropical, half-legendary islands. It contrasts them with modern, progressive New Zealand and Australia. It gives you an idea of something most of us never see.

I might remind you that in the Southern Hemisphere the seasons are the reverse of ours. Thus, if you leave the United States in December or January, you will be literally "sailing into Summer." And it's quite a sail.

To the romantic — I give you the South Seas!

South America

Perhaps the best way to see our nearest continent-neighbor is also by cruise. South America is too big to visit on a regular monthly sailing and expect to see much worthwhile. There are regular cruises along both east and west coasts that pre-select what you will see. You may not like having other people do your picking and choosing — but it does save time and money.

The phrase "time and money" is only comparative, of course. You can't hope to go to South America unless you have a good share of both. But for the honeymooning couple who have the necessary wherewithal, South America seems to me about as interesting as any place you could possibly visit. As in Mexico, big things are happening to the way people live and think in South America. A trip there will give you not only an unsurpassed variety of new sights and scenic grandeur — it will give you the feeling of being "in on" a new, perhaps momentous chapter of history.

Travelers to South America need passports, incidentally. This is the first time I've had occasion to mention it, for all other places mentioned so far dispense with this formality for American visitors.

Europe

So much has been written about Europe that it would be idle for me to attempt any exhaustive additions. In the little space available, about all I can do is remind you that, if you have the price, the possibilities for a European honeymoon are infinitely attractive and almost infinitely varied.

One thing to remember is that Europe has well-defined seasons and that travel follows them rigidly. Thus Winter sees the visitor active in the Alpine snows or sunning himself along the shores of the Mediterranean. Summer opens up the endless appeal of France and Germany, England and Scotland and the Scandinavian states. "Trade follows the flag" — but in Europe travel follows the sun.

If your honeymoon budget permits an Atlantic crossing, don't miss stopping in London and Paris no matter where you may be headed. The big European capitals are fascinating at any season. So are the smaller towns. History, geography, art, architecture, picturesque customs — but why go on? Europe is the travel mecca for most Americans and it's certain that I can't tell you anything new about it. When you actually get ready to discuss the matter — see your travel agent.

See him, too, about the really *long* cruises — around Africa, around the world. The latter may last as long as six months, and are almost always conducted during the Winter and Spring. Seeing India, Singapore, the Red Sea, the South Pacific, the Mediterranean — there is the perfect combination of honeymoon and education, all in one package.

Such things are a far cry from Cape Cod and Michigan and Florida, the simple near-to-home honeymoons we talked about earlier in this chapter. But it doesn't matter what you do or where you go, provided you can afford it. And provided you make pretty sure in advance that you will *enjoy* it.

Remember — whether your groom has a hundred dollars or ten thousand to spend, there is a honeymoon *somewhere* to suit his bride!

CHAPTER XXIII

Photographs—from the Journalistic Angle

THAT HORROR of the press from which many people used to suffer — the feeling that there is something disgraceful in having one's picture in the society columns of the newspapers — is largely a thing of the past. So Our Bride today takes it quite as a matter of course, if her family is important, and her wedding is to be a large affair, that her photograph in her bridal attire will appear in the newspapers the day after the wedding, and sometimes even the photograph of the whole bridal party. Weddings are popular news; everybody likes to read about them; and the families concerned in the wedding should be willing, within reason, to cooperate with the press. Moreover these clippings are mighty entertaining to read in after years!

In the case of families not well known in a large city, from the newspaper point of view there is not much news in the wedding, unless it be a mere statement of the fact; and those concerned should not feel injured if the affair does not gain much attention. Newspaper space is very limited these days, and all editors are hard put to it to use even a proportion of the news that is legitimate. But in the case of a big and important wedding, it is the newspapers which do the seeking.

To meet all the requests from the press for detailed information in regard to an important wedding, to provide photographs, to answer questions, is no small task. Sometimes a member of the family may take this duty upon herself — or himself. In such an event a typewritten tabulation of the important data regarding the wedding gown, costumes of the wedding party, special features of the ceremony, names of important and out-of-town guests and other information saves a lot of talking and is a boon to the society writer or editor, who will then fix the "story" to suit himself, and give it whatever space he thinks it worth. Nothing is more agonizing to a society editor than the painstaking hand-written flowery account of a wedding written by someone not familiar with the correct style for newspaper reporting.

If no such useful member of a family is available, the family of the bride whose wedding is a matter of considerable public interest may engage a sort of "public relations" person, perhaps a former society editor or reporter, to handle these details. No bride wants to read a description of her wedding gown as crepe de chine when it was satin, or have it said that the decorations were chrysanthemums when they were lilies! This method will save many errors. *The photographs of Our Bride in her wedding gown should be taken preferably, as we have said, on the day of the final fitting.* Then they will be ready for the newspapers or for the fashion or society magazines, if requested. Newspapers and magazines are usually very careful to "honor" release dates. Thus though Our Bride may give her picture to a certain society editor a week before her wedding, she may be very sure that it will not appear until after the wedding, if it is marked as released at a certain hour on the wedding day.

Pictures of the bridal party usually have to be taken on the day of the wedding itself — perhaps after the reception, just before the bride and groom leave to change for their honeymoon. If the occasion is sufficiently important, newspaper photographers and even newsreel camera men may be present, and every courtesy should be extended to them within reason. In addition formal photographs will probably be taken by a special photographer engaged by the family. Then the group photographs or the photographs of the bride and groom will be available as gifts to relatives, and also for society magazines that may request them.

Since large city newspapers go to press very early, the material for the society pages is to a large extent prepared the day before. Thus information on the morning wedding, if it is to be reported in the afternoon papers, should be in the hands of the editor before the ceremony takes place. An afternoon wedding will usually be reported first in the same day's evening papers. In a smaller city, where papers go to press later, data on the wedding may not be obtained by a reporter or given to him until the ceremony actually takes place. But any cooperation that the families of the bridal pair, in the case of an important wedding, can extend to the society editor, who lives a pretty hectic life anyway, is always greatly appreciated, not only by himself, but by the entire staff.

CHAPTER XXIV

Invitation and Announcement Forms

INVITING THE GUESTS

WE HAVE already, as in the case of Amelia's small formal wedding, considered the use of the handwritten, informal invitation. Let us now consider the engraved invitation. The use of this depends more upon the size of the wedding and of the wedding budget than upon whether the affair is formal — that is, with the bride wearing wedding gown and veil; or informal — with the bride in afternoon gown and hat or similar costume.

In the case of a formal wedding as large and expensive as the Beverley-Wood affair described in Chapter IV, where many mere acquaintances are invited, engraved invitations must of course be used. Generally when other than relatives or friends of the family are bidden, this method of invitation is more suitable. One does not telephone or send informal notes usually to mere acquaintances on an occasion of this kind. To most weddings of any size held in a church, unless taking place in a smaller community and considered a sort of "neighborhood" affair, guests are usually invited by engraved invitation.

In the engraved invitation itself, there is perhaps less variety permissible than in any other detail of the wedding arrangements. Invitations must be "just so" as to wording, and forms are quite rigid.

STYLES OF ENGRAVING

We see very frequently what is called "London Script." Today there are other styles of engraving which are preferred by many — and which are most attractive and easily read — an important item. Of these the two most popular are "English Script" and "shaded Roman." The shaded Roman is charged for by the letter and the other two are charged for by the line.

Let us look at these three kinds of engraving together, so that we may have them clearly in mind:

Mr. and Mrs. Schuyler Warren Wood

(ENGLISH SCRIPT)

[111]

Mr. and Mrs. Schuyler Warren Wood

(LONDON SCRIPT)

Mr. and Mrs. Schuyler Warren Wood

(SHADED ROMAN)

There are also several other types of engraving popular nowadays, though perhaps not so frequently used. They are, "lined Roman," "solid Roman," "Norman" and "Trinity Text." They appear thus:

Mr. and Mrs. Schuyler Warren Wood

(LINED ROMAN)

Mr. and Mrs. Schuyler Warren Wood

(SOLID ROMAN)

Mr. and Mrs. Schuyler Warren Wood

(NORMAN)

Mr. and Mrs. Schuyler Warren Wood

(TRINITY TEXT)

A folded white or ivory sheet of fine quality paper, usually vellum or what is known as "wedding plate," is used for wedding invitations and announcements. There are a variety of correct sizes, according to preference, with enclosed cards in sizes to correspond; any first class engraver knows what is correct. The invitation or announcement proper occupies only the first page. The others are always blank. Usually the lettering is set within a "panel." A family crest, if used, should be embossed without color. Enclosed cards are of the same "stock" and style of engraving as the invitation.

For mailing wedding invitations, there are two envelopes — an inside and an outside. The inside envelope contains the invitation and accompanying cards; it is left unsealed. Only the title and last name of the person or persons receiving the invitation are written on this envelope — thus "Miss Brown" or "Mr. and Mrs. King." It is inserted so that the side with the name faces the flap of the outer envelope.

The names of the whole family are not included on the same invitation. Mr. and Mrs. George Willington will receive one invitation, with inside envelope addressed to "Mr. and Mrs. Willington." Their daughter will receive an invitation with the inside envelope addressed to "Miss Willington," and the outer one to "Miss Jessica Willington," and another invitation will go to their two sons, both envelopes being addressed to the "Messrs. Willington." Names of streets and names of states should always be spelled in full; no abbreviations should appear on a wedding invitation except "Mr." and "Mrs."

It is, however, possible, if deemed wise in order to save expense, to address the outer envelope to "Mr. and Mrs. George Willington," and the inner to "Mr. and Mrs. Willington and family." But "and family" is never put on the outside envelope.

Typical Invitation Forms

Let us now consider the invitation to a wedding such as that of Marie Louise Wood. There are two possible forms for this invitation; let us see each form.

The following form, using the more personal "your presence" is preferred by many people:

Mr. and Mrs. Schuyler Warren Wood
request the honour of your presence
at the marriage ceremony of their daughter
Marie Louise
to
Doctor Martin Gordon Beverley
on Tuesday, the tenth of June
at half after four o'clock
at Saint Giles Cathedral
in the City of New York

And here is the second form, in which the name of the prospective guest is written in longhand in ink:

Mr. and Mrs. Schuyler Warren Wood
request the honour of

Miss Marie Coudert Brevurg's

presence at the marriage ceremony of their daughter
Marie Louise
to
Doctor Martin Gordon Beverley
on Thursday, the tenth of June
at half after four o'clock
at Saint Giles Cathedral
in the City of New York

⟦ 113 ⟧

Note the "honour of" in the invitation to the marriage ceremony and the spelling; this wording is preferred today.

Enclosed with the first invitation is the reception card reading thus — (note that for the reception, the "pleasure of your company is requested"): —

Mr. and Mrs. Schuyler Warren Wood
request the pleasure of your company
on Thursday, the tenth of June
at five o'clock
at the Hotel Ascot

The favour of a reply is requssted to
Eleven hundred Fifth Avenue

The card for the reception in the second instance reads thus:

Mr. and Mrs. Schuyler Warren Wood
request the pleasure of

Miss Marie Coudert Brennig's

company on Thursday, the tenth of June
at five o'clock
Hotel Ascot

R.S.V.P.

Enclosed in either invitation, as the wedding ceremony is in a large city church, is the church admittance card. In both instances it will read, in the same style of engraving as the invitation:

Please present this card
at Saint Giles Cathedral
on Thursday, the tenth of June

If the pew is to be designated, "Pew No.   " may be engraved in the lower left hand corner, the actual number to be written in ink.

If the wedding reception is to be very large and the guests at the marriage ceremony are to be few — the reverse of the case in the Beverley-Wood wedding, — the reception becomes the chief part of the wedding invitation and the invitation to this will occupy the folded sheet, while the invitation to the ceremony will be on an enclosed card, — (let us suppose that Marie Louise Wood's parents had issued five hundred invitations to the church and one thousand to the reception.)

The following would be the reception invitation:

Mr. and Mrs. Schuyler Warren Wood
request the pleasure of your company

The Store's Part
IN YOUR WEDDING

Mᴀʏ we remind you that the Strawbridge & Clothier Store has played a material part in the success of many thousands of weddings? Brides of 1868 and later years have told us of the gleaming satins, laces, linens and other things bought here for that happiest occasion of their lives.

In other pages of this book we have described some of the services we hope to render, not only to make *your* wedding a success, but to provide for your home many things in which you will find long-lasting joy and satisfaction. Here are other things of importance which you may confidently depend upon us to supply:

Iɴᴠɪᴛᴀᴛɪᴏɴs ᴀɴᴅ Aɴɴᴏᴜɴᴄᴇᴍᴇɴᴛs — Our Engraving Department is equipped to execute orders for all the forms favored by Miss Brennig, of the highest possible quality at each of the various prices.

Tʜᴇ Bʀɪᴅᴇ's Sɪʟᴠᴇʀ — A fine selection of new designs in Sterling Flatware, to be chosen in such assortments and quantities as desired; also Sterling Tea Sets and other "hollow-ware" in variety — and, of course, the better grades of Silver-plated ware.

Hints for the Groom

The bride may, very properly, suggest this store as a good place at which to buy the Engagement Ring as well as the Wedding Ring, and whatever jewelry gifts he may have in mind for best man and ushers, as well as for the bride.

He may be reminded, also, that correct wedding clothes and all accessories for himself may be bought here with assurance of satisfaction.

STRAWBRIDGE & CLOTHIER
Market, Eighth and Filbert Sts., Philadelphia

at the wedding reception of their daughter
Marie Louise
and
Doctor Martin Gordon Beverley
on Thursday, the tenth of June
at five o'clock
at the Hotel Ascot
in the City of New York

Kindly send response to
Eleven hundred Park Avenue

And following would be the enclosed card to the ceremony:

Mr. and Mrs. Schuyler Warren Wood
request the honour of your presence
at the marriage ceremony of their daughter
on Thursday, the tenth of June
at half after four o'clock
at Saint Giles Cathedral
in the City of New York

If the marriage ceremony and reception both take place at the house, with only a small number of guests at the ceremony, the card will be smaller; reading thus:

Ceremony at half after four o'clock

But when the number of guests at a home marriage ceremony and reception are the same, there need be but one invitation on the folded sheet — requesting "the pleasure of your company at the marriage."

Combination invitations to both the marriage ceremony and reception on the same sheet are not in the best of taste.

AT HOME CARDS

An At Home card may be enclosed with the wedding invitation, saying merely, since the bride-to-be has not yet acquired her married name:

At home
After the first of August
Seventy Five Park Avenue
New York City

SPONSORSHIP OF THE WEDDING INVITATION

Naturally if only one parent of the bride-to-be is living, the invitation to her wedding is issued under the one parent's name. If she is an orphan, her nearest male relative should issue the invitation — thus a brother, a grandfather, an uncle, with the name of his wife included, if he has one. In lieu of a male relative, a sister, preferably one who is married, or an aunt, may issue the invitation, including the name of her husband. In either of these cases, or in the case of another relative or friend issuing the invitation, as the name of the bride-to-be is not the same as her own, she will use her last name with "Miss" prefixed. Thus, if Marie Louise Wood's married aunt had issued her invitations, they would have read:

Mr. and Mrs. James Walsingham
request the honour of your presence
at the marriage ceremony of their niece
Miss Marie Louise Wood, etc.

Train Cards

Sometimes in the case of a very large and expensive country wedding, the family of the bride will engage a special train or a special car, leaving a station at a certain time. They will then enclose with the wedding invitation a card reading thus:

A special car will be attached to train
leaving South Station, Boston
at 2.55 P.M.
Returning train leaves Brookline for
South Station, at 6.30 P.M.
Please present this card in place of ticket

Sometimes, when there is no special train, it saves guests trouble to enclose for their reference an engraved card bearing train information. However, so many people travel by motor these days that train cards are not so often used.

Typical Announcement Forms

The rules for announcing the wedding, as far as sponsorship is concerned, follow the rules of the wedding invitation. Naturally those who have been invited to the ceremony or the reception will not receive announcements. They should be mailed on the day of the ceremony, but not until it is actually performed!

The style of engraving selected will of course be the same as that chosen for the wedding invitation. The hour of the ceremony is not included, since that is unimportant once the ceremony is over. The year, however, is spelled out in full.

When parents are making the announcement, the following is the correct form; it is of course, like the invitations, on a folded white or ivory sheet of fine quality paper, usually vellum or what is known as "wedding plate."

Mr. and Mrs. Schuyler Warren Wood
have the honour of announcing
the marriage of their daughter
Marie Louise
to
Doctor Martin Gordon Beverley
on Thursday, the tenth of June
one thousand nine hundred and thirty-three
at Saint Giles Cathedral
in the City of New York

They may also use a form which merely says "announce the marriage of" instead of "have the honour of announcing." But parents like the first form usually — for to have their daughter happily married is indeed an honour!

If the bride and groom are sending out their own announcements for any reason as heretofore explained, following is an example — let us suppose that Marie Louise Wood has announced her own:

Doctor Martin Gordon Beverley
and
Miss Marie Louise Wood
announce their marriage
on Thursday, the tenth of June
One thousand nine hundred and thirty-three
in the City of New York

With the announcements may be enclosed an At Home card, which will use the married name of the bride and groom. The card is of course in keeping with the announcement as to size and style of engraving. The most formal wording follows:

Doctor and Mrs. Martin Gordon Beverley
will be at home
after the first of August
Seventy-five Park Avenue
New York City

CHAPTER XXV

From My Letter File

I HAVE TRIED, in previous chapters, to provide solutions for the majority of the special problems that may confront Our Bride and Groom in planning their wedding. But there are many special and unusual situations which may arise that no general discussion of weddings could cover. It is quite probable that such questions may still occur to those who read this book.

Each year hundreds of letters come to me from all over the country, asking me what to do in particular situations. It may be that you, Bride and Groom, will find among some of these an answer to some question still unsolved. I shall therefore choose from among these hundreds of letters a few that are especially interesting, and note the answers I have made to them:

CEREMONY AT FIANCÉ'S HOME

"My parents are dead, and I therefore room and board. My fiancé's parents have a nice home and they want the wedding there. Is this possible? Of course I shall pay the expenses, and it will have to be a simple wedding as I shall have only a small amount to spend. Would you suggest my brother giving me away? How many attendants should I have? Where should I have the reception — at my fiancé's, or at my aunt's? . . . "

Since I can sense that you really wish to be married in your fiancé's home, it is a perfectly proper place under the circumstances, for your wedding. Have the reception there also. Your eldest brother is the rightful person to give you away. One attendant for such a wedding is sufficient. . . .

A WEDDING IN A FRIEND'S HOME

"I am a widow and I am shortly to be married to a widower. My best friend is the wife of an army general, and she is an invalid. She is very anxious for me to be married in her apartment, as she cannot leave home. Could we with propriety go to their home for the wedding ceremony, inviting about a dozen friends? They live near. What hour and attire would you suggest? . . . "

You most assuredly could be married with propriety in your friend's home. Your guests should be invited, of course, by your host and hostess. An afternoon gown, possibly of chiffon, print or crepe with hat and accessories to match, would be appropriate. Perhaps if your friend is an invalid, a simple afternoon wedding would be best. Your wedding announcements should be issued by yourselves. . . . (See Chapter on Announcements.)

RECEPTION WITH INFORMAL WEDDING

"I am to be married informally at St. Thomas Chapel at three o'clock. What type of reception should I have and where? The majority of guests will be from out of town. They may not have time to change into afternoon dress. I do not want those who do not have time to freshen up from travel to be embarrassed. . . . "

Must you be married at three o'clock? Could you not make it four? Then I would suggest an informal tea reception immediately following in the small ballroom of a hotel, which is often used for just such an affair. . . .

WEDDING PROCESSION FROM A BALCONY

"Our church has a balcony all the way around upstairs, except across the front, and stairs lead down onto the pulpit platform from each side. Would it be all right to have the bridesmaids (two or three), the matron of honor, the flower girl and the bride come down the stairs? Should the ushers come down the aisle nearest the bridesmaids? . . ."

I think this would be a most unusual and beautiful wedding procession. The ushers had best come down the middle of the aisle of the church. The minister, best man, and groom will, of course, come out of the vestry door at the further side of the pulpit platform, if possible. . . .

A DECEASED BRIDE'S WEDDING GOWN

"My fiancé's father has offered me his wife's wedding dress. She died over a year ago, and I knew her slightly. The dress is perfectly beautiful, trimmed with rose point lace, and very little would have to be done to it. I know that he wants me to wear it very much, but he does not want me to feel obligated to do so. Personally I should love to wear it, but I wonder just what the etiquette is. . . . "

Your acceptance of his offer is not only a very lovely gesture for you to make, but it is quite within the realms of good taste. . . .

BUSINESS SUITS FOR USHERS AT A FORMAL WEDDING

"I am to be married this summer in a church in a white gown and veil. But in our small college town, cutaways and silk hats are not usually worn.

Would it be possible for the groom and ushers to wear some other type of attire besides cutaways? . . ."

Under the circumstances, as you have explained them to me, though cutaways are the correct attire for a formal afternoon wedding — under which heading yours comes, since you are wearing gown and veil — it will be good taste for both groom and ushers to wear white flannels and dark blue coats, appropriate ties, and black shoes. . . .

Throwing the Wedding Bouquet

"Must I throw my wedding bouquet to my bridesmaids? I should like to give it to my mother. . . . "

While it is customary and a pretty ceremony for a bride to toss her bouquet when she is halfway up the stairs — if there are stairs! — if you want to present it to your mother, there is no reason why you should not do so, and I am sure your bridesmaids will offer no objection. . . .

The Bride Writes Her Invitations

"I am twenty, and I expect to be married soon in our apartment. My mother is an invalid and cannot help me in the wedding preparations; she is not able to write the invitations. Would it be correct for me to send out informal notes and how shall I word them?"

Under the circumstances, it will be quite proper for you to write your own invitations. You might say something like this:

Dear Jean:

I am to be married to Carey James on Thursday, June eighth, here in our apartment. Mother and I both hope that you can come. It will be so nice to have you with us.

Sincerely,

Elsie

A Black Wedding Gown?

"Some time ago I read in a New York paper that a very smart bride wore a black wedding gown and veil with black accessories. I have a complexion which looks very well in black, and I think black is very chic. What is your opinion of my wearing this type of wedding gown? . . ."

Personally I think the idea of black for a wedding gown the most absurd, ridiculous and unsuitable idea I have ever heard. Black is known as the color for mourning — at least in our country. Why should any bride want anything so lugubrious and so emblematical of sorrow at a wedding, which is supposed to

*be the very embodiment of joy and confidence for the future? People who indulge
in such costumes are only looking for publicity. . . .*

Reception After Registry Marriage

"I am to be married by a civil magistrate. What should I wear? I should
like to have a small reception afterward. Would this be correct and where
could I have it? . . ."

*If you go to the office of a magistrate, the most appropriate costume would be
street wear suitable to the season. You may quite properly have a reception,
but it should be of the most informal kind. If you live in the place where your
marriage will take place, the reception should preferably be in your own home
regardless of its size. Otherwise, you might have it in the home of relatives; or of a
friend; or if this is not possible, in the small dining-room of a hotel. . . .*

Flower "Fads"

"Bracelet bouquets have been suggested to me as an attractive and novel
way of wearing flowers with my bridal gown, a bracelet on each wrist. With
these, I understand, I would carry a prayer book. Is this correct? . . ."

*Such things as "bracelet bouquets" — on each wrist, or on only one wrist —
are quite permissible — and a prayer book is then often carried as a finishing
touch to the costume. Like muffs of tulle for bridesmaids, however, flowers on the
wrist are more a fad of the moment than in lasting favor. The two bracelet idea
is better suited to the formal wedding gown; one flower bracelet would be more
appropriate with a "garden party" costume, and no prayer book would be
carried. . . .*

A 17 Year Old Maid of Honor

"I am to be married at a church wedding. I should very much like to have
my young sister, aged seventeen, as my maid of honor. Is she too young for
this? . . ."

*If your sister has sufficient poise and presence for such a post in your wedding
procession, there is no reason why she should not be maid of honor. Many young
girls of seventeen these days have all the poise and coolness in the world. Age
makes no difference in choosing your maid of honor. . . .*

Going Away Costume for Traveling

"We are spending our honeymoon at an exposition in a middle western
city and are going by motor from New York. Will you give me suggestions
as to the costume I should wear for the trip? . . ."

Sport clothes should be worn for such a journey as you mention. For example, a woolen jersey dress, with a smart tweed coat; or a tweed suit with a smart and becoming sweater and a sport hat to harmonize, would be quite suitable. . . .

Using Costumes Already on Hand

New Brunswick, Canada

"My daughter plans to be married quietly in February, and we have had difficulty in getting her a really nice suit to be married in. She has a lovely white French lace dress trimmed with a band of dark brown fox fur; it has a cape effect. Would this costume be entirely out of place if she were to be married in church, and what sort of hat, shoes, stockings and gloves should she wear with it? She also has a black afternoon dress with a bright red top. Would this be suitable? At the last moment, she may be able to get a nice navy blue suit. If so, what should she wear with this and what kind of flowers should she carry? . . ."

Of the two costumes already on hand, I should certainly choose the French lace dress; black, no matter how brightly trimmed, even in an informal costume, is too gloomy for a wedding. With the French lace dress, she might wear a hat of felt or of white straw cloth material; with perhaps a nose veil; white crepe sandals, "nude tone" hose, French suede white gloves (elbow length); and instead of carrying flowers, she should wear a corsage, which might be of white orchids or gardenias. . . .

If she is able to have the navy blue costume and you decide on that, suggested accessories for it would be a gray satin blouse, gray navy rough straw or felt hat; gray French suede gloves, navy or black kid oxfords or pumps with modish tone hose on the grayish brown hue. A corsage of white orchids or gardenias might be worn on the shoulder. . . .

Small Church Wedding Party

Pullman, Wash.

"I am to be married some time this spring at a small church wedding. The church will accommodate about two hundred guests. Would four ushers, four bridesmaids, a maid of honor and best man be sufficient for the wedding party? . . ."

Four bridesmaids, and a maid of honor and best man would be quite enough for the wedding you are planning. If you expect to have enough guests to fill the church, however, four ushers might have some difficulty in seating them promptly. It might be advisable, in this case, to have two additional ushers; there need not, as we have said before, be the same number of ushers and bridesmaids. . . .

[122]

Bride May Walk Alone

"My father has been dead for many years, and for various reasons, I cannot choose among my uncles to give me away. Would it be right for me to walk to the altar alone?"

Under the circumstances it is quite correct for you to walk to the altar alone. If your church regulations require you to be given away, your mother, aunt, uncle, sister or other near relative could, at the proper moment, step from his or her pew on the left hand side of the aisle and perform this ceremony. . . .

A Time Table of Wedding Plans

LET US ASSUME, by way of illustration, that Our Bride and Groom have set the date of their wedding for the 30th of June; have decided where it shall be and how large; that Our Bride knows what she can spend; and that three months is available for completing the wedding plans. This is the ideal period. Let us see now how the various items of preparation may be fitted into these three months.

If two months only are available for the wedding preparations instead of three, it is very simple to combine the work of the first four weeks with that of the next four. Naturally the table holds good for any time of year.

THE BRIDE'S TIME TABLE

April 1–15	Decide on general plans for your wedding.
(1st two weeks)	Begin compiling the family guest list.
	Draw up a tentative budget according to the sum you have decided upon.
	Itemize necessary purchases, according to their proper percentages.
	Confer with engraver, florist, caterer, orchestra. Obtain estimates.
April 15–30	Obtain the guest list from your fiancé's family.
(2nd two weeks)	Make a list of your personal friends and his.
	Check all lists together, as to possible duplicates.
	Invite your bridesmaids and ushers.
	Begin shopping for linen, lingerie, flat silver.
	Start shopping for wedding costume and personal trousseau.
May 1–15	Complete the guest list.
	Order the invitations.
(3rd two weeks)	Place orders for your personal trousseau, and wedding costume.
	Have the first fittings on wedding costume, and trousseau.
May 15–31	O.K. estimates and plans of florist, caterer, orchestra.
(4th two weeks)	Have invitations addressed, stamped, sealed, ready for mailing.
June 1–15	Mail all invitations at beginning of this period.
	Complete all shopping.
(5th two weeks)	Have a final fitting of your wedding gown now if possible.
	Arrange for your photographs to be taken at the final fitting.
	Record and acknowledge wedding gifts as they arrive.
June 15–30	As many idle days as possible! A few idle days insure a happy wedding day.
	Rest!

Assure delivery of all trousseau purchases one week before wedding
    date.

Rest!

Bridesmaids' dinner or luncheon. Present their gifts.

Rest!

Tea for viewing of gifts.

Rest!

Groom's bachelor dinner.

Rest!

June 29th — Dinner to bridesmaids and ushers.
           Rehearsal.
           So, to bed early this night!

June 30th — the Wedding Day — with everybody calm and
    happy.

Costumes at a Glance

THE FORMAL WEDDING — SPRING, SUMMER, AUTUMN OR WINTER — MORNING OR AFTERNOON

Bride: Formal wedding gown in white, off-white or pastel shade, the mode following the fashion. Material according to the season, Spring or Summer, satin, mousseline de soie, chiffon or other soft material. Autumn or Winter, satin, velvet, moiré silk, and so on. Train, one to seven yards in length; short or long sleeves; kid or suede gloves if short sleeves; neck high in back, in front as décolleté as desired, if in keeping with the place of the ceremony. Veil of tulle, or all lace, or chiffon, of length and type desired, with lace cap, or cap of same material as veil, or veil fastened to head with orange blossoms; shower or arm bouquet of white flowers, or with a little color if desired.

Groom: Cutaway coat of oxford tone cheviot cloth. Spring or Summer, light gray, white, or buff linen waistcoat. Autumn or Winter, waistcoat or vest same material as coat or of gray or buff suede-cloth, with gray striped worsted trousers, gloves; "bat wing" collar, pearl gray Ascot tie or four in hand or bow tie of black and gray stripes; white handkerchief folded so that one inch of white shows in coat pocket; boutonnière usually lilies of the valley from bride's bouquet; top hat; plain crooked handle malacca cane with silver or gold band below handle with engraved initials, if so desired.

Maid or Matron of Honor: Costume always a contrast to or complementing that of the bridesmaids. Spring or Summer, lace, net, chiffon, crepe, organdy or any sheer material in prevailing mode; hat in keeping with the gown, gloves worn if sleeves are short; slippers matching hat or gown; bouquet to complement gown. Autumn or Winter, velvet, flat crepe, satin and similar materials. Colors: blue, brown, red orange, green and so on.

Bridesmaids: Costumes to complement or harmonize with each other, and with honor girls. Spring or Summer, light pastel shades in lace, net, chiffon, crepe or any sheer material in prevailing mode; hats in keeping, large or small as desired, to match or harmonize with gown. Autumn or Winter — velvet, flat crepe, satin and so on, hats of same or contrasting materials; slippers matching gowns, gloves when sleeves are short or as finishing touch to costume; bouquets to blend with general color scheme.

Best Man: Cutaway coat, gray striped trousers. Spring or Summer —

light gray, buff or white linen waistcoat; white sailcloth spats, white doeskin gloves. Autumn or Winter, buff or gray suede-cloth vest, or matching material of coat; tie optional, collar usually "bat wing"; boutonnière may be like ushers', or different; top hat, malacca cane as groom, if desired.

Ushers: All attired exactly alike — cutaway and striped gray trousers like groom and best man; "bat wing" collars; vests, spats, gloves, ties all uniform — similar or different from those of best man; top hat.

Flower Girls (if any): Kate Greenaway costumes or "party frocks"; Autumn, Winter — faille silk, velvet and so on; colors to blend with scheme of wedding. Spring or Summer, chiffon, similar soft material. Small Colonial bouquets with Kate Greenaway costumes; with party frocks, baskets of flowers or small bouquets.

Women Guests: Afternoon type costumes with hat and gloves, slippers, purse, all harmonizing. Spring or Summer, chiffons, plain or flowered, laces or crepes or other light materials; Autumn or Winter, darker tones in velvet, satin, flat crepe, lace. Corsage if desired worn on left shoulder.

Men Guests: Cutaway coats of oxford tone cheviot; gray striped worsted trousers. Spring or Summer, white, gray, or buff linen vests; Autumn or Winter, dark gray suede-cloth waistcoats, or same material as coats; four in hand, bow or Ascot ties, gloves, top hat.

Mothers of Bride and Groom: Afternoon type costume, in colors that will complement the gowns of the wedding party, since they must stand nearby in receiving line. Spring or Summer, light materials; Autumn or Winter, darker tones of velvet, satin and so on. Hat, gloves and slippers to harmonize; corsages.

THE FORMAL EVENING WEDDING

Bride: Wedding gown in formal afternoon or semi-evening mode, with accessories as in formal wedding any other time of day. Full evening mode for bride wearing veil not in best of taste.

Groom: Full evening attire: — tail coat, stiff white bosomed shirt, "bat wing" collar, white piqué bow tie, white vest, trousers with satin stripe, same material as coat, evening shoes, black silk socks, white kid or doe skin gloves; top hat. Style of stick optional.

Maid or Matron of Honor: Formal afternoon or evening gown, possibly with headdress if it is necessary with costume, or theatre-type hat. Most churches require "head covering" on women.

Bridesmaids: Formal afternoon or evening gowns, in variety of colors, headdresses, if necessary, like that of maid of honor, or theatre-type hat.

Best Man: Full evening attire, as groom with exception of boutonnière.

Ushers: Full evening attire, as groom with exception of boutonnière.

Flower Girls: Party dresses, or Kate Greenaway costumes with bonnets; bouquets or baskets of flowers.

Mothers of Bride and Groom, Women Guests: Evening attire, "head covering" in church, if required.

Men Guests: Full evening attire.

The Formal Garden Wedding — Any Time of Day
Spring or Fall

Bride: Same as in summer formal wedding.

Groom: Cutaway as in summer formal wedding. White linen waistcoat, white doe skin gloves. White sail cloth spats.

Maid or Matron of Honor and Bridesmaids: Same as in Spring or Summer formal wedding. Dresses may be more informal in style of material, gloves may or may not be worn, even with short sleeves; hats may be of the garden variety if worn; bouquets of garden flowers are attractive.

Best Man: Same as groom with exception of boutonnière and tie.

Ushers: Same as groom with exception of ties and boutonnières.

Flower Girls: Same as in Spring or Summer formal wedding.

Mothers of Bride and Groom: Same as formal church wedding in Summer, only lighter tones and perhaps larger hats.

Women Guests: Same as in Summer or Spring formal wedding.

Men Guests: Dark blue coats, white flannel trousers, if desired; or formal afternoon attire — (See costumes for formal wedding.)

The Informal Garden Wedding

Bride: "Garden party" costume of chiffon, plain or flowered, lace, crepe, organdy or other similar materials. Hat of modish size harmoninizing with gown; bouquet as desired; gloves optional. (Sometimes no hat at very simple garden wedding.)

Groom: Dark blue coat, white flannel trousers, black and white shoes or all white, or all black, no gloves, boutonnière.

Maid or Matron of Honor: Garden party costume or costume as in any summer informal wedding.

Bridesmaids: Same as in any summer informal wedding; without gloves if desired; usually hats.

Flower Girls: Party frocks, of mull, net, linen — bonnets or hats, or wreaths of flowers; bouquets or baskets of flowers.

Mothers of Bride and Groom: "Garden Party" costumes in light shades; large or small hats, usually corsages.

Women Guests: Afternoon gowns of light color, hats, gloves optional.

Men Guests: Dark blue coats, white flannel trousers, black oxfords.

INFORMAL WEDDING AT HOME, CHURCH, HOTEL — ANY TIME OF DAY

Bride: Afternoon costume of material suitable to season, with appropriate hat, shoes, gloves, usually corsage. Or traveling costume of material suitable to season, matching accessories, and corsage.

Groom: Sack suit, light or dark color depending on time of year and type of honeymoon; derby, straw hat or fedora, gloves, stick. Cutaway, with correct accessories, if hour of day and formality of bride's afternoon gown demands such.

Maid or Matron of Honor or Witness: Informal afternoon costume, hat, accessories.

Bridesmaids: Usually none at most informal weddings. If bridesmaids, they should be dressed in keeping with honor girl.

Best Man: Same type clothes as groom.

Ushers: Usually none. If ushers, same type clothes as groom.

Mothers of Bride and Groom: Informal afternoon costumes — or street costumes.

Men Guests: Similar to groom and best man — sack or business suits.

REGISTRY OFFICE OR RECTORY WEDDING

Bride: Street costume with hat usually. In country district, might wear afternoon frock with hat.

Groom: Sack suit, accessories as in preceding wedding.

Women Witnesses or Guests: Street or informal afternoon costumes.

Men: As groom.

———————

NOTE. — Exceptions may be made to an accepted rule and still remain within the bounds of "the correct" when they are carried out with consistency of detail, particularly in reference to the groom's and other male members' attire in a formal wedding party. For the formal daytime wedding at any time of year, the following may be substituted for the cutaway coat and striped trousers: dark business suit, preferably blue; white shirt, starched collar; four-in-hand tie of appropriate coloring; black oxfords; black socks; boutonnière; no spats or gloves. For the formal daytime wedding in warm weather only: white linen or white gabardine suit, or dark blue or gray coat with white or gray flannel trousers; white shirt; white shoes or a combination of white-and-black or white-and-brown when white suits or white trousers are worn; white socks preferable; four-in-hand tie of appropriate coloring; boutonnière; no spats or gloves.

The Bride's Gift Record

NOTE:

Suggestions regarding the use of this Gift Record
will be found in Chapter XVI under the heading
"Gifts to the Wedding Pair"

NO.	NAME AND ADDRESS OF DONOR	RECEIVED	DESCRIPTION OF GIFT
1	Mr and Mrs. W. Banning Cedars, Del.		Living Room Day Sofa
2	W. Howard Banning Cedars, Del		Brass Candle she
3	Mr and Mrs. Robin Brooks Fishers Island, Ny		Check Hooked rugs
4	Mrs. Aldrich Purry 416 Montezuma Rd., Coradale, Ala.		Living Room lamps – white
5	Mr and Mrs. Willard Haas Marshallton, Del		Two large Symphony Irg. spro
6	Misses Jane Sarah and Esther Haas		Georgean glass pieces.
7	Mr and Mrs. Clifford Simpson Marshallton, Del		White Linen Lunch e Tatting
8	Misses Simpson and Billy Simpson		Georgian glass pieces
9	Mr and Mrs. Harry Bracken and Harry Junior – Devmond, Del		Georgian Bon Bon Dish
10	Mrs Lafette Thompson Mr. Raymond Thompson		Fruit dish
11	Mr and Mrs. Howard Best Misses Helen, Dede and Buddy		Fisher Island a Copper bowl
12	Miss Laura Suter 52 Oneca St. Narwich, Conn		Olive gask and sugar tongs Syrup

The Bride's Gift Record

WHERE GIFT WAS PURCHASED	ACKNOWLEDGED	PERSONAL REMARKS

NO.	NAME AND ADDRESS OF DONOR	RECEIVED	DESCRIPTION OF GIFT
13	Mr. Will Hoffman, Chads Ford, Pa.		Hand lace piece
14	Hercules Powder Company - Friends		Complete toast master
15	Mr. and Mrs. Lammot duPont, Saint Amour, Wil. Del		Symphony Sterling
16	Mr. and Mrs. Henman, Duncan, Miss Mary Duncan.		Tilt Top living room table
17	Mr. and Mrs. Earle Ewing, Cedars, Delaware		Georgian glass piece.
18	Mr. and Mrs. Alton Bradway, 1605 Lincoln St. Wil, Del		Sterling cream and sugar set
19	Miss Sandy Packs, Washington St Wil		clock
20	Mr. and Mrs. Thomas E. Jeffers, Stanton, Del.		Symphony sugar spoon
21	Mr. and Mrs. Will Mitchell, Cranson Heights, Del		Olive dish and stirling fork
22	Capt. and Mrs. Alonza, Fishers Island, N.Y.	McKown	Six Symphony butter knives & demi tasse
23	Mr. and Mrs. Elrood, Elsmer, Del	Robinson	Georgian glass pieces
24	Mr. and Mrs. Charles Gallagher, Cedars, Del.		Silver coffee Set

The Bride's Gift Record

WHERE GIFT WAS PURCHASED	ACKNOWLEDGED	PERSONAL REMARKS

NO.	NAME AND ADDRESS OF DONOR	RECEIVED	DESCRIPTION OF GIFT
25	Mr. George Pyle Miss Doris Pyle, Cedars		Kitchen spice set and baskets
26	Mrs. Magdelene Gaccnutt Rising Sun Lan Wil Del		Sterling cake plate
27	Mr. and Mrs. Paul Schussel 605 Spruce St. Wil, Del		Lace table cloth
28	Mr. and Mrs. John Conley Rising Sun Lan Wil Del		Yellow living Room sofa pillow
29	Mr. and Mrs. Owen Dougherty 607 West 27th St. Wil, Del		Table cloth
30	Miss Nancy Henry Rising Sun Lane Wil.		White large table cloth
31	Miss Esther Eby Miss Hannah Pugh		American set of dishes
32	Mr. and Mrs. Harry Immon Rising Sun Lane, Wil		Bread tray
33	Mrs. Annie Ryon Mrs. Herbert Dinsmore		Georgian glass piece
34			
35			
36			

The Bride's Gift Record

WHERE GIFT WAS PURCHASED	ACKNOWLEDGED	PERSONAL REMARKS

NO.	NAME AND ADDRESS OF DONOR	RECEIVED	DESCRIPTION OF GIFT
37			
38			
39			
40			
41			
42			
43			
44			
45			
46			
47			
48			

The Bride's Gift Record

WHERE GIFT WAS PURCHASED	ACKNOWLEDGED	PERSONAL REMARKS

NO.	NAME AND ADDRESS OF DONOR	RECEIVED	DESCRIPTION OF GIFT
49			
50			
51			
52			
53			
54			
55			
56			
57			
58			
59			
60			

The Bride's Gift Record

WHERE GIFT WAS PURCHASED	ACKNOWLEDGED	PERSONAL REMARKS

NO.	NAME AND ADDRESS OF DONOR	RECEIVED	DESCRIPTION OF GIFT
61			
62			
63			
64			
65			
66			
67			
68			
69			
70			
71			
72			

The Bride's Gift Record

WHERE GIFT WAS PURCHASED	ACKNOWLEDGED	PERSONAL REMARKS

The Bride's Gift Record

NO.	NAME AND ADDRESS OF DONOR	RECEIVED	DESCRIPTION OF GIFT
73			
74			
75			
76			
77			
78			
79			
80			
81			
82			
83			
84			

The Bride's Gift Record

WHERE GIFT WAS PURCHASED	ACKNOWLEDGED	PERSONAL REMARKS

The Bride's Gift Record

WEDDING EMBASSY YEAR BOOK

NO.	NAME AND ADDRESS OF DONOR	RECEIVED	DESCRIPTION OF GIFT
85			
86			
87			
88			
89			
90			
91			
92			
93			
94			
95			
96			

The Bride's Gift Record

WHERE GIFT WAS PURCHASED	ACKNOWLEDGED	PERSONAL REMARKS

The Bride's Gift Record

NO.	NAME AND ADDRESS OF DONOR	RECEIVED	DESCRIPTION OF GIFT
97			
98			
99			
100			
101			
102			
103			
104			
105			
106			
107			
108			

The Bride's Gift Record

WHERE GIFT WAS PURCHASED	ACKNOWLEDGED	PERSONAL REMARKS

NO.	NAME AND ADDRESS OF DONOR	RECEIVED	DESCRIPTION OF GIFT
109			
110			
111			
112			
113			
114			
115			
116			
117			
118			
119			
120			

The Bride's Gift Record

WHERE GIFT WAS PURCHASED	ACKNOWLEDGED	PERSONAL REMARKS

NO.	NAME AND ADDRESS OF DONOR	RECEIVED	DESCRIPTION OF GIFT
121			
122			
123			
124			
125			
126			
127			
128			
129			
130			
131			
132			

The Bride's Gift Record

WHERE GIFT WAS PURCHASED	ACKNOWLEDGED	PERSONAL REMARKS

The Bride's Gift Record

NO.	NAME AND ADDRESS OF DONOR	RECEIVED	DESCRIPTION OF GIFT
133			
134			
135			
136			
137			
138			
139			
140			
141			
142			
143			
144			

The Bride's Gift Record

WHERE GIFT WAS PURCHASED	ACKNOWLEDGED	PERSONAL REMARKS

NO.	NAME AND ADDRESS OF DONOR	RECEIVED	DESCRIPTION OF GIFT
145			
146			
147			
148			
149			
150			
151			
152			
153			
154			
155			
156			

The Bride's Gift Record

WHERE GIFT WAS PURCHASED	ACKNOWLEDGED	PERSONAL REMARKS

NO.	NAME AND ADDRESS OF DONOR	RECEIVED	DESCRIPTION OF GIFT
157			
158			
159			
160			
161			
162			
163			
164			
165			
166			
167			
168			

The Bride's Gift Record

WHERE GIFT WAS PURCHASED	ACKNOWLEDGED	PERSONAL REMARKS

NO.	NAME AND ADDRESS OF DONOR	RECEIVED	DESCRIPTION OF GIFT
169			
170			
171			
172			
173			
174			
175			
176			
177			
178			
179			
180			

The Bride's Gift Record

WHERE GIFT WAS PURCHASED	ACKNOWLEDGED	PERSONAL REMARKS

The Bridal Party

BRIDE

Beatrice Martha Banning

GROOM

Robert Eldridge Brooks

BEST MAN

Thomas Porchon

MAID OF HONOR

Mary Totnall Duncan

MATRON OF HONOR

_____

BRIDESMAIDS

_____

_____

_____

_____

BRIDESMAIDS

_____

_____

_____

_____

USHERS

_____

_____

_____

_____

USHERS

_____

_____

_____

_____

FLOWER GIRLS

_____

_____

PAGES

_____

_____

RING BEARER

_____